SPACE AND SOCIETY 5
LAND USE AND DEVELOPMENT

SPACE AND SOCIETY 5

LAND USE AND DEVELOPMENT

Andrew Kirby and David Lambert

LONGMAN

Acknowledgements

We are indebted to Penguin Books Ltd for permission to reproduce the 'Epilogue' from pp. 304–306 R. E. Pahl *Whose City?* Copyright (c) R. E. Pahl, 1965, 1966, 1967, 1968, 1969, 1970, 1971, 1974, 1975.

We are grateful to the following for permission to reproduce photographs:

British Petroleum, pages 74 and 75; Findus, page 73, Brendan Hearne, page 71; International Press Agency, page 72; *Punch*, page 59; United States Department of Agriculture, page 76.

LONGMAN GROUP LIMITED
*Longman House, Burnt Hill, Harlow, Essex CM20 2JE, England
and Associated Companies throughout the World*

© Longman Group Limited 1985

First published 1985
ISBN 0 582 35355 6

Set in 10/11pt Baskerville, Linotron 202

*Published by Longman Singapore Publishers (Pte) Ltd
Printed in Singapore*

Contents

Preface

To the teacher

Aims

This series is designed for use within the sixth form as a back-up to the now familiar texts such as Tidswell's *Pattern and Process in Human Geography*, Bradford and Kent's *Human Geography* and Haggett's *Modern Synthesis*. We have designed the books as 'readers', that is, free-standing volumes that elaborate on particular topics, fleshing out the bare bones introduced within the textbook by presenting extracts from original sources and illustrative exercises. The latter are particularly important, as the emphasis throughout the series is upon the practical application of ideas, models and theories, rather than the abstract discussion of such deductive concepts. In this sense, the aim is to use the student's existing experiences of the 'real world' as a foundation for investigation, in order that these can be channelled into a systematic understanding of basic geographic principles.

Organisation

This book can be used in three ways. It is intended for use as a whole; in other words, the student should be able to use both the practical material and the original extracts in approaching a particular topic. In some instances, however, this may not be required. In such cases, it should be possible to use the practical examples alone, or if required, the published extracts as reference material.

Within each volume, a standard format is used. The authors' text is interspersed with secondary material, and at the end of each section there are questions, a check-list and notes which are designed to highlight the key issues that have been introduced. The latter are referred to throughout the text.

To the student

This book is one of a series of geography 'readers'. This means that the aim of the series is not to provide a complete source of facts and information for your sixth-form course; instead the intention is to provide a firm grounding in some of the fundamental ideas within the subject.

You should aim to read the volumes in the series as a back-up to your course. If you have problems in understanding some sections, discuss them with your teacher. There are, however, check-lists of key issues at the end of each chapter which you should refer to, and many of the ideas will become clearer as you work through the examples.

1

The mesh of economic development

1.1 Introduction

So far in this series, we have introduced four topics. In the first two books, we considered two key geographical principles: the way in which space is transformed into regions, and the way in which space is a medium within which various phenomena interact. The second pair of books dealt with that key aspect of contemporary society, the city; we examined the difference *between* cities (in terms of size, function and form) and also the differences *within* cities, concentrating upon the way in which urban areas have evolved historically.

In this volume, we deal with an even more basic concept, which we can identify as the process of economic development (ED): by this we mean the way in which the process of production takes place in different locations: internationally, nationally, within urban areas and in rural areas. ED is thus the study of the many individuals and organisations which exploit natural resources, create employment and generate wealth. ED is, of course, therefore explicitly geographical, because the pattern of production is not uniform: the existence of ED is usually responsible for social change and economic benefit, whereas the absence or decline of ED usually results in economic and social decay. (*Notice*: this focus upon ED is therefore narrower than the process. of national economic and social development, which is used in discussion of 'the least developed countries': this is explained more fully in the Key issues. In short, we are emphasising development *within* countries, not the development *of* countries.) In this chapter, we will begin by defining what we mean by the economic development process, and then how ED takes place in a geographical context. Development first.

1.2 The historical evolution of the economic development process

In book 4, we examined the evolution of cities in an historical context, and in that evolution we identified particular, distinct phases such as pre-industrial, industrial, and corporate capitalist (the creation of large firms with many different interests). Each of these periods represents a particular form of the ECONOMIC DEVELOPMENT process, which has altered steadily over the last three centuries.

1. Pre-industrial

The movement from primitive to advanced society has occurred in many different ways: language, behaviour and intellectual capabilities have all changed. These intellectual developments have happened in many contexts (art, literature etc.) but particularly in terms of the ability to manipulate the natural environment. From early attempts to construct shelters through to the most recent ability to create artificial life, there has been a consistent urge to recreate order from the resources of the environment.

The ways in which human development have come about are enormously difficult to explain. If we examine the issue globally, we are aware that different societies have evolved along similar paths, but in subtly different ways and – most interestingly – at very different times. The Chinese, for example, possessed sophisticated technology at a time when Europeans lived in conditions of superstition and deprivation. Why does the relationship between society and change evolve as it does? Why did Chinese society then begin to stagnate intellectually at the very time that European cultural evolution was accelerating? The numerous different factors which would account for this and other changes make a simple explanation virtually impossible to find. As Mario Cippolla shows in his study of the improvement of clocks, it was frequently a whole series of circumstances that encouraged a particular individual or group of experimenters to work on a project: and once one invention appeared, it might then find uses in totally unconnected fields. In short, it is clear that from the sixteenth century onwards, developments in the sciences and the arts constituted a shifting dynamo within (European) society, without there being a particular universal goal for this progress.

2. Industrial – capitalist

Sometime in the eighteenth century, a shift occurred in the economic development process. As we shall see, most observers agree that something happened in Britain shortly before the Napoleonic wars that produced a very different economic system, and as result, a very different type of society.

In short, the change was the introduction of a factory system, taking individuals from the land where they had well-defined tasks and roles, and placing them in new locations where their labour could be bought and sold in many different ways. This had happened already in towns, where apprentices had worked with craftsmen; here however we see a very different *scale* of things. The factories were large; they used various types of power to work machines (principally water, then steam). Workers were numerous, and had to find shelter where they could: sometimes in new settlements built specially by the factory owners (such as Saltaire or Bournville).

Most importantly, the nature of society changed. For centuries, European society had been rigidly ordered: aristocrats and the church had constituted the power of government, with a sprinkling of merchants and wealthy landowners contributing to small parliaments. Wealth was based in the main upon the holding of land, and what could be taken above and beneath it; others made in turn their fortunes from the distribution of primary products (like wool) or the goods required by the affluent (dyes, reading matter, spices).

Within this ordered society there emerged a new breed, whose wealth stemmed from the production of the new industrial goods – the machines, the railway lines, the armaments – that marked the industrial age. These capitalists created wealth by paying for their workers' labour, but charging buyers a premium for the goods that they purchased. The temptation was to pay very small wages, and charge high prices – thus creating large personal fortunes. Names familiar today – William Randolph Hearst, Andrew Carnegie, and others – established their fortunes as the nineteenth century progressed.

The shock that this provided to the social system was enormous. In an agricultural society, change is slow: production is predictable. Town and country have closely-defined economic roles. Suddenly, a capitalist society dictated change. More production meant bigger profits. More profits meant more capital, that could be invested in more and newer enterprises. More profits meant more men with power: first economic, then social, then political. In a very brief time, the balance of social relations shifted from the land to the factory, from the country to the town, from the aristocracy to the capitalist.

3. Corporate – capitalist

If pre-capitalist society was essentially stable, then the capitalist age is essentially *unstable*. The instabilities show themselves in many ways. Most important is the necessity to keep labour costs and the overall costs of production as low as possible: in addition, it is important that capital is used and reused, in order that the maximum financial returns are made.

We have already seen some of the results of these necessary forces. The development of suburban housing (discussed in book 4) was in part a way of opening up new areas to house construction, a profitable and large industry. Other tendencies are reflected in broader social changes. As already argued, industrialisation was soon accompanied by the creation of rich and powerful families. These in turn created powerful industrial combines, and one of the most startling changes in society is the way in which enormous companies like ICI, ITT, General Motors and Standard Oil (Esso) have emerged, with extremely wide industrial interests. Most importantly, these combines do not base themselves in one town or even one region any longer. The urge to reduce the costs of production means that their holdings are spread across countries and across continents. In short, these giant companies (rightly called 'multinationals') have spread the process of capitalist economic development right across the world: their economic power (some have annual turnovers which exceed the gross domestic product of countries with the wealth of Belgium) ensures their ability to operate virtually anywhere, including the non-capitalist countries like the Soviet Union (see Key issues).

1.3 The process of economic development

The three-fold scheme outlined above is of course only a simplification of a highly complicated process. What we have done here is to emphasise the change from a pre-capitalist society to one based upon a widespread circulation of capital.

A detailed scheme of social and economic change has been produced by Rostow, who identifies *five* particular stages in the national development process, as it might apply to a particular country.

(a) *the traditional society*: 'one whose structure is developed within limited production functions, based on pre-Newtonian science and technology' (1960, p. 4)

(b) *societies in the process of transition*: 'the preconditions for take-off (see below) were initially developed in Western Europe of the late seventeenth and eighteenth centuries as the insights of modern science began to be translated into new production functions in both agriculture and industry' (1960, p. 6)

(c) *take-off*: 'during the take-off, new industries expand rapidly, yielding profits a large proportion of which are reinvested in new plant: and these new industries in turn stimulate, through their rapidly expanding requirement for factory

workers, the services to support them, and for other manu-
factured goods, a further expansion in urban areas and in
other modern industrial plants' (1960, p. 8)

(d) *the drive to maturity*: 'the stage in which an economy demon-
strates the capacity to move beyond the original industries
which powered its take-off and to absorb and to apply ef-
ficiently over a very wide range of its resources – if not the
whole range – the most advanced fruits of (then) modern
technology' (1960, p. 10)

(e) *the age of high mass consumption*: 'it is at this stage that resources
tend increasingly to be directed to the production of
consumers' durables and to the diffusion of services on a
mass basis . . . the sewing machine, the bicycle and then the
various electric-powered household gadgets were gradually
diffused. Historically, the decisive element has been the
cheap mass automobile with its quite revolutionary effects –
social as well as economic – on the life and expectations
of society' (1960, p. 11).

1. Examine Rostow's outline of the national development process.
   Attempt for a country like Britain to date each of the phases
   through which it has passed.

2. Can you imagine any situations in which this progression might
   be altered: can you think of any countries which have altered
   the order of change?

3. Can you apply Rostow's model to the real world, and identify
   particular countries which fit the five different stages, including
   those still at the first stage?

Discussion

As we can see in figure 1.1, Rostow has charted quite specifically
the dates at which various countries have approached and reached
'take-off'. As we can also see, Britain had a long-start upon other
European countries, who in turn have had a head start upon the
rest of the world. In the main, the progress towards maturity and
mass consumption has been linear, although note that both Canada
and Australia, countries with enormous natural resources and very
small populations, reversed slightly their development histories.

One of the major problems with Rostow's model is this assumption that national development is a rigid phenomenon, and that all
countries must evolve in the same way. Also worrying is the im-
plicit assumption that all countries will ultimately achieve a take-
off of their own.

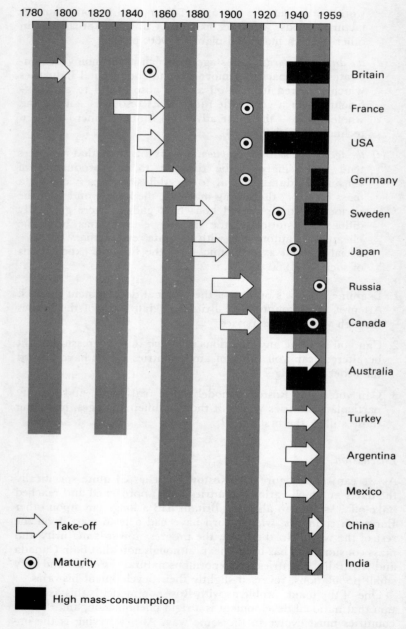

Figure 1.1   The process of economic take-off and the dates it was reached by different countries (after Rostow)

.4 The world economy model

Rostow's model of national development is not geographical: in other words, he has not considered the inter-connections between different countries. Economic take-off is not confined within a nation's boundaries: it involves a trade process with other countries. Historically, advanced nations have involved poorly-developed (pre-take-off) countries in the capitalist system: either by colonialisation (as happened in the last century) or by investment (via multinationals at present). This might be taken as evidence that these poorer countries experienced accelerated progress: this is however not the case. The drive to reduce costs and maintain levels of profitability has encouraged many large combines to invest in non-developed nations. This does not necessarily improve the economic position of the latter.

The map in figure 1.2 contrasts the distribution of population and income throughout the world. A major disparity exists between the so-called 'core' nations and the rest of the market societies: the former possess an excess of five times the income, with only 40 per cent of the latter's population. What is particularly worrying is the way in which these disparities are predicted to maintain. Figure 1.3 shows the global levels of unemployment prediction, broken down into the advanced and non-developed states. It can be seen that unemployment is likely to rise within both groups, but also that the *proportions* in the non-developed countries will be enormous, with only very small working populations supporting very high levels of non-production. The recognition of the existence of a world economy is very important to our argument, which is:

'the economic development system is explicitly geographical: it organises space in order to maximise profitability, with the result that a shifting pattern of economic development (and its corollary, decline) occurs.'

1. Consider what is meant by 'the economic system' in this chapter. Note that in figure 1.2 other economic systems are mentioned: is this quotation likely to apply in these countries?

2. What is meant by the 'organisation of space', and who is doing the organising?

3. What is meant by 'development' and 'decline': how would we best measure these?

Discussion

In this chapter, and indeed throughout this book, we will concentrate upon the capitalist system: as we will show in chapter 5, other

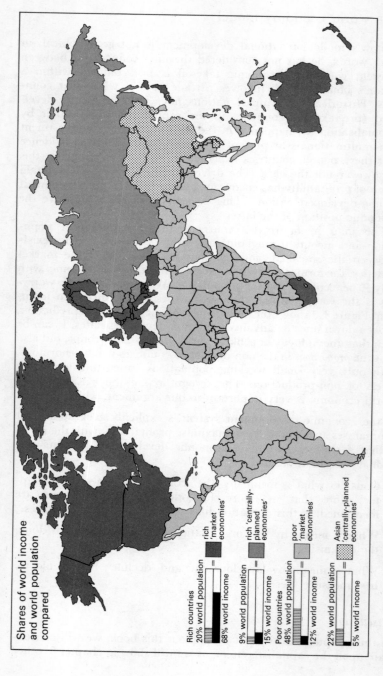

Shares of world income
and world population
compared

Rich countries
20% world population =
68% world income

rich
'market
economies'

9% world population =
15% world income

rich 'centrally-
planned
economies'

Poor countries
48% world population =
12% world income

poor
'market
economies'

22% world population =
5% world income

Asian
'centrally-planned
economies'

Figure 1.2 The relationship between world income and world population (from Kidron and Segal, 1981)

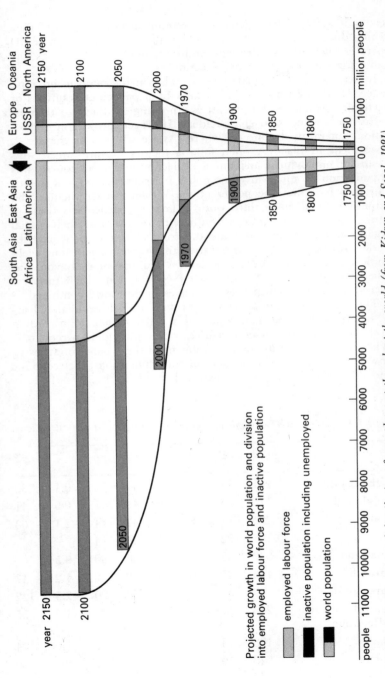

Projected growth in world population and division
into employed labour force and inactive population

■ employed labour force

■ inactive population including unemployed

■ world population

Figure 1.3   The projected distribution of unemployment throughout the world (from Kidron and Segal, 1981)

economic systems exist (such as communism in China), and they exhibit different tendencies. At present, the capitalist system of ED operates increasingly through multinational firms, who, as the name suggest, operate in many countries.

It is these multinationals who are able in the main to organise space. It is they who can invest heavily in particular countries or particular regions within countries. In doing so, they create prosperity for workers and shareholders. However, growth in one location can mean decline elsewhere. As we will see in chapter 2, investment in place A often follows factory closures in B: this means unemployment and financial decline. Often, of course, this organisation of space involves political issues. As yet, the multinationals have not the power of the Western governments, who actually created many third world countries (particularly those in Africa) in the nineteenth century: here there was an explicit spatial organisation in order to create the colonial ties so beneficial for trade. However, there is no question that these corporations wield immense economic muscle: the largest multinational, Exxon, has sales that amount to $7 million *per hour*, and its 1978 turnover exceeds that of the 70 poorest countries in the world combined.

The measurement of poverty is always a difficult problem. Clearly, we can talk about poor countries in different senses, in relation to *economic* measures, *social* measures or even individual perceptions. What is so pressing about the problems of these poor countries is, however, that their poverty exists in both dimensions, the economic and the social. This is well illustrated in table 1.1

Table 1.1   Indicators of economic and social wellbeing for 31 poorest nations

	1	2	3	4	5	6	7	8
Afghanistan	241	12		2.6	41	15	0.1	90
Bangladesh	118	26	8	3.0	49	11	0.9	41
Benin	224	11	8	2.9	47	14	−1.1	68
Bhutan	103	22		2.1	44	4		
Botswana	632	33		2.0	56	30	9.5	
Burundi	146	25	10	2.0	42	2	1.2	17
Cape Verde	160 GNP	37	10	1.9	57	20	−2.3	122
Central African Republic	248	7	8	2.2	44	41	−1.2	55
Chad	188	15	8	2.0	41	18	−1.0	24
Comoros	248	59		2.3	46	12	−2.1	59

	1	2	3	4	5	6	7	8
Ethiopia	143	15	9	2.1	40	15	0.4	20
Gambia	244	6		2.8	41	18	0.4	84
Guinea	62	20	5	2.9	44	18	0.6	87
Guinea-Bissau	250	5		1.5	41	24	0.0	58
Haiti	278	24		1.7	53	28	2.3	66
Laos	83	28		1.4	42	14	−2.1	102
Lesotho	145	52	2	2.3	51	5	1.3	
Malawi	175	25	12	2.8	47	10	4.7	70
Maldives	147	70		2.5	46	11	11	
Mali	131	10	6	2.5	43	20	0.1	30
Nepal	119	19		2.2	44	5	0.3	14
Niger	220 GNP	8	10	2.8	43	13	1.5	48
Rwanda	188	16	15	2.8	47	4	1.1	30
Somalia	130 GNP	60	7	2.3	44	30	1.4	78
Sudan	320 GNP	20	6	2.6	47	25	0.5	141
Tanzania	263	66	9	3.4	52	12	0.2	53
Uganda	280 GNP	25	6	3.0	54	12	−3.1	39
Upper Volta	126	2	14	1.6	43	9	−0.8	29
Western Samoa	520	99		0.8	65	21		
Yemen Arab Republic (AR)	447	13	5	1.8	42	10	2.2	73
Yemen People's Democratic Republic (PDR)	316	27	11	2.3	45	37	3.5	545

Titles for columns in the table

1 Gross Domestic Product (GDP) per head, 1978. Figures in US$.
2 Adult literacy rate, 1976. Figures are % of adults aged 15 and over able to read and write.
3 Manufacturing as a share of GDP, 1979. Figures in %.
4 Average annual growth of population, 1970–79. Figures in %.
5 Life expectancy at birth, 1979. Figures in years.
6 Urban population, 1980. Figures in % of total population.
7 GDP per head growth rate, 1970–79. Figures in %.
8 Energy consumption per head, 1979. Figures in kilograms of coal equivalent.

(Source: Geofile, 1982)

1.5 Conclusions

In this chapter we have attempted to outline the nature of economic development, and the ways in which the economic system creates patterns of wealth and poverty.

What is particularly important to understand is that the international system of inequalities has direct parallels: in terms of regional inequalities within particular countries, and even the ways in which other types of land-use are organised, such as within cities, or in rural areas. In each case, we are interested in the way in which economic interests are involved in the most profitable organisation of space.

In this chapter, we have talked a little about industrial concerns. Let us now examine industrial behaviour in greater detail.

Key issues

ECONOMIC DEVELOPMENT In this book, the emphasis is upon the way in which economic activities function across the landscape. By economic activities, we mean any process which is involved in the creation of profit: this therefore includes industries, agriculture, the construction of buildings, and so on. This also means that we are focusing upon economic activities within *capitalist* societies. Note that there is a large difference between economic development which goes on *within* a geographical area, and the overall economic progress *of* that area. We are used to thinking in terms of countries becoming developed, but this can be misleading. Consider the case of the Middle East oilfields. Countries with large oil exports are clearly wealthy; however their capital is invested abroad in places like Europe. There is often little real economic development in these countries themselves. In such a case we would say that the countries were developing, but there was little ED.

VODKA – COLA TRADE Although we are used to thinking of the large political differences that exist between East and West (countries like the USSR on the one hand and the USA on the other), we should not assume that there is no trade between them. The governments themselves trade commodities like grain (USA to USSR), and in order to pay for this, the socialist countries have allowed multinationals to operate within their boundaries. Firms like Coca-Cola and Fiat are happy to make their products behind the 'Iron Curtain' because the labour is cheap and highly disciplined there.

2

Industrial location and regional problems

2.1 The location of the firm

In this chapter, we will examine the process of economic development (ED) at the regional scale. We are particularly interested in trying to explain the ways in which different regions in a country like Britain or France enjoy contrasting standards of living, with some regions suffering from many problems: high unemployment, poor housing quality, low spending on education, and so on: (these issues were discussed in book 1, *The Region*). Naturally enough, many of these problems stem from the fact that the industrial base of the local economy is weak, and this in turn reflects the fact that industrial activities have not located in the region, or have moved away. To understand why this occurs, we need some simple model which will suggest why firms make locational decisions.

2.2 Weber's model of industrial location

One of the oldest models in this context is Alfred Weber's. Despite being produced in 1909, it is still widely used as a method of thinking about industrial location. The basics of the model are outlined in the three diagrams that constitute figure 2.1.

In the first diagram, we introduce a resource landscape. At different locations, there exist different mineral sources (M1 and M2) plus 'points of consumption': these might be other firms, or markets of consumers. Weber assumed that firms would require basic resources, which would be processed, turned into goods and resold – to individuals or other firms. Thus there are *two* locational decisions. How far should the factory be from the minerals or similar inputs, and how far should the market be from the factory?
1. Suggest an industrial process which conforms to Weber's view i.e. one which involves two basic inputs and one output.
2. Identify whether your product *loses* or *gains* weight during manufacture.
3. Try to predict where the factory should be located.

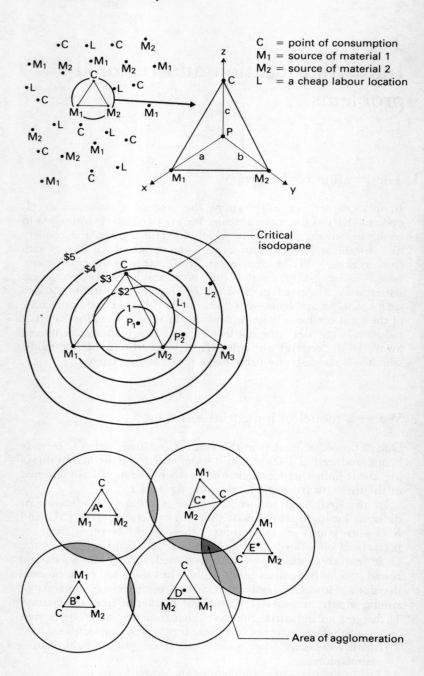

Figure 2.1   Weber's analysis of the firm (from Weber, 1929)

Discussion

Weber, living in an era of heavy industry and relatively poor transport communications, emphasised the importance of minimising the costs of moving both inputs and outputs. As we can see from figure 2.1, we can decide the best location for the factory by constructing a triangle, joining M1, M2 and C. Our factory is to be located at processing point P. The location to P can be solved algebraically, by solving the following equation:

$$\text{minimise } ax + by + cz \tag{1}$$

where a is the distance from P to M1, b from P to M2 and c from P to C; and the quantities x, y and z are tonnages. Probably an easier way to solve the problem is to think of the lines connecting P as strings with weights attached. The weights are proportional to the tonnages involved. So, if the raw materials involved are very heavy, we can imagine the strings being pulled toward M1 and/or M2. Conversely, if the processing at P involves a weight *gain*, then the strings will be pulled up towards the top of the triangle, and P will be closer to C, the market.

Most industrial processes involve a weight loss, notably when raw materials are involved. Thus steel production consists of turning heavy inputs (coal, ore) into a slightly less bulky product, steel. In consequence, the original steel producers were located on ore or coal fields. Conversely, some processes involve a weight gain: brewing is perhaps the classic example. Because relatively light ingredients are transformed by the addition of water, historically most breweries were highly localised, and the remnants of this system can be seen in the existence of ancient breweries like Brakspear's in Henley on Thames and Theakston's at Masham.

The brewing example reminds us of Weber's emphasis upon transportation, and thus his antiquity. Increasingly, modern economics depends less and less upon transport costs, and more and more upon factors such as labour or economies of scale. These were just assuming importance at the turn of the century, and Weber offers additions to his model in order to take them into account. In the second diagram, for example, a source of cheap labour is introduced at L1. The way that this is evaluated is as follows:

(a) investigate the increase in transport costs incurred by moving the factory away from P. This is done by working out the additional cost per item of production; as we can see, it is possible to map the additional costs, using what Weber called *isodapanes*;

(b) locating at L1 will save $3 per unit produced, due to cheap labour. As we can see, L1 is within the $3 isodapane. Thus a relocation of P will involve an increase in transport costs but an overall saving in labour costs. Thus, a relocation, to P2, is desirable.

Similarly, Weber realised that many firms do not operate in an isolated manner; in other words, they have close ties with the firms that buy their products. If these interlinked companies make locational decisions together, then they can make overall savings, and this is illustrated in the third diagram. There, Weber shows that these economies of scale can be exploited geographically: his example requires that three firms agglomerate, with the result that firms, C,D, and E can be seen to have the possibility of relocating close together in order to make savings.

2.3 Industrial location and regional development

We have already suggested that Weber's approach reflects the times during which he wrote. In recent decades, industrial location decisions have been influenced by rather different considerations: first, because transport costs have become a great deal less important, and second, because additional factors have entered the locational equation.

In the period immediately after the Second World War, a concentration of industrial development occurred in the South East, the West Midlands and the East Midlands. New light engineering firms did not require the resources offered by the old industrial cores in Wales, Scotland and the North East. The attractions of the new industrial areas was such that governments were forced to introduce 'regional policies', designed to encourage firms to locate at least some of their activities in the peripheral regions: these policies were outlined in book 1. Regional aid became additionally important in the late 1960s, when further changes in the economy appeared; since 1955, the steady decline in manufacturing employment has ultimately become a rapid contraction, with 1.7 million jobs (21 per cent of the 1955 total) disappearing by 1980.

The basic results of these changes are shown in figure 2.2. Here, we can see the changes in manufacturing employment for the period 1971–76, plotted for sub-regions in the UK.

1. Examine the manufacturing employment changes in figure 2.2. Identify three types of sub-region: first, those experiencing major losses; second, those experiencing minor losses; and third, those experiencing employment gains.

2. For the three types of area that you have identified, can you suggest why there has been this type of change over the 1971–76 period?

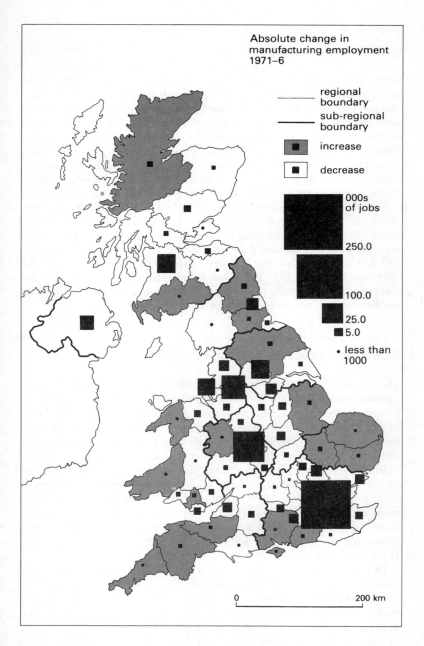

Figure 2.2   Changes in manufacturing employment 1971–76, for sub-regions in the UK (from Keeble, 1981)

Discussion

Studies of employment change over the period 1966–76 show consistent results. Most important, manufacturing enterprises have been ridding themselves of labour. This means that in what have become the new industrial cores – the South East and the Midlands – there have been heavy job losses. The reason that these areas seem to have done badly, compared with traditional centres of unemployment, is to be found in the operation of regional policy. Thus sub-regions in East Anglia, parts of Wales and the South West have received new jobs which compensate for contractions in existing firms. Regional policy has also of course been in operation in the old industrial hearth areas, like the North East and Central Scotland, although here continued job loss has only partially been offset by new employment creation. David Keeble, an economic geographer, has emphasised the key role that has been played by regional policy, which is generally assumed to have created nearly 400,000 jobs: he writes 'at the broad interregional scale, the evidence indicates that the most important single influence upon current manufacturing location trends is government industrial location policy' (Keeble, 1976, p. 287).

2.4 Industrial location decisions in the 1980s

The evidence provided by Keeble might seem to show that locational decisions in the industrial sphere are now heavily influenced by government policies, and that this therefore has beneficial implications for ED at the regional scale in Britain. However, the story is not quite this simple. Whilst it is true that regional policy has restricted growth in the new core areas and produced some redirection of jobs to the periphery (and the same has happened in the field of services), it is probably fair to argue that many of these jobs would have been located there anyway, with or without regional policy incentives. In order to understand this, we need to focus upon the decision-making criteria now employed by large corporations: as we shall see, these are very different from those applicable in Weber's time.

In figure 2.3, we focus upon what has been termed 'the corporate interface'. This lies between the trends within the economy, and the geographical decisions taken by the firm. In the 1980s, the macro-economic trend is essentially a story of falling returns, which implies one message for industry: a reduction in costs. This occurs in various ways, but most simply by reducing labour and increasing technological inputs within production.

The decisions that corporate actors will take at this point will

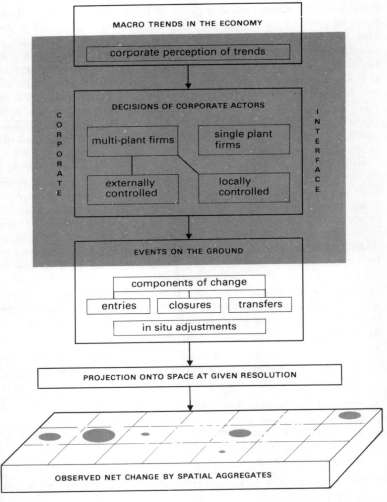

Figure 2.3   The relationship between economic trends and geographical patterns (after Lloyd and Reeve)

> *In this diagram, the authors suggest how we might study industrial geography. First we examine the basic trends within the economy (growth, decline etc.). Then we examine the decision-making process within the individual firm: this will include all its constituent parts, all the different plants, and so on. These decisions will have geographical implications: expansions, takeovers, factory closures. It is these processes that we know best as basic industrial geographic patterns.*

vary; if the firm has only one plant, it might make labour redundant, or even relocate. If it is a firm with several sites, it will probably aim to transfer some of its activities to an area with large supplies of relatively cheap labour, such as can be found in the peripheral regions. Regional policy grants are helpful, but industry is really seeking poorly-skilled, low-paid, part-time labour. In an era of high technology production, these workers can perform relatively sophisticated tasks at low cost. Moreover, if the firm changes its production strategies, it is relatively easy for it to close down the site and relocate elsewhere: perhaps in the UK, perhaps in another country entirely.

In terms of ED at the regional scale therefore, we can see that the jobs created in places like Scotland and Wales do not involve high rates of pay, and may even do nothing to change unemployment rates, as many of the people employed may not have had the opportunity to work before. Conversely, highly-paid jobs are remaining within the core regions: the headquarters, advertising, distribution and research activities of large corporations all tend to be concentrated in the more prosperous regions. This is due to INERTIA, the fact that these functions benefit from economies of agglomeration, and the reluctance that highly skilled labour shows when asked to move to a depressed area. The degree to which these types of functions are geographically concentrated is emphasised in figures 2.4 and 2.5.

1. Examine the maps of American corporations (of the sort outlined in chapter 1), and identify the basic geographical distributions.

2. Account for the different concentrations visible:
   (*a*) the Great Lakes;
   (*b*) New York – Boston;
   (*c*) the south, including Texas;
   (*d*) the West coast.

3. Examine the map of European headquarters, and again identify basic patterns.

4. Contrast the patterns visible in Britain or France with those in evidence in Germany, for example.

Discussion

These two maps tell us a great deal about contemporary ED. In the American case, we can see four types of headquarters location. First, there are those corporations which maintain a presence in the New York – Boston – Philadelphia axis, despite the high costs and

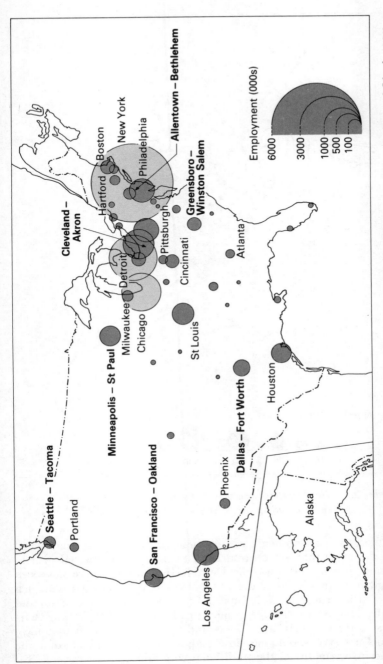

Figure 2.4 Headquarters' locations of the leading 500 industrial corporations in the USA, 1973 (from Dicken and Lloyd, 1981)

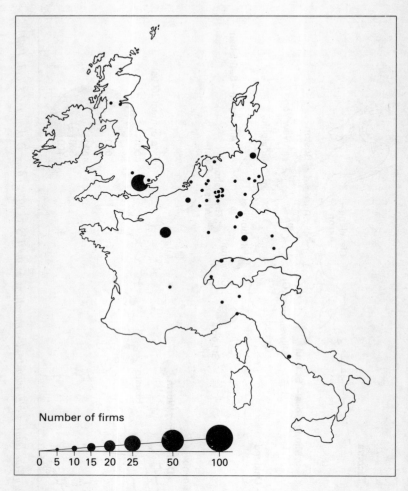

Figure 2.5   Headquarters' locations of the leading 100 industrial corporations in the EEC, 1974 (from Lee, 1976)

unpleasant environments within these cities. These are paralleled by the firms that are centred close to the main industrial hearth, which remains in cities like Detroit. In contrast, there has been growth in what is called the 'SUN-BELT' – that broad expanse which stretches across from Carolina to Texas, and on into Colorado and California. As we can see, some firms have moved their headquarters to the sun-belt, and Texas and California in particular have benefited. We should not lose sight of the fact though that the epicentre remains in the traditional core areas.

In the European context, we see rather different patterns. Britain and France display very high concentrations, which reflects the economic primacy of London and Paris respectively. In contrast, German industry is far more dispersed, with headquarters being clustered in the Ruhr, in Frankfurt, in München and in Hamburg, which reflects in part the disruption and subsequent reconstruction in the immediate post-war years.

The net effect then of these changes is summarised by two economic geographers, Peter Lloyd and Peter Dicken (1981).

recent locational trends in corporate organisation arise from the pressures of the competitive environment at international and national scales . . .. The precise response to such pressures obviously varies from one firm to another. Commonly however it involves efforts to reduce labour costs and to get rid of old and obsolescent capital equipment and buildings . . .

In deciding how to organise their operations geographically, firms are faced with a spatial surface of opportunities and constraints. This is a multifaceted surface, made up of spatial variations in resources and materials, suppliers and customers, capital availability and labour availability . . .

Whatever the detail of the corporate processes, the effects on employment may be felt in two ways. First, there may be changes in the *number* of jobs provided from place to place, and, second, there may be changes in the *types* of jobs available . . .

Quite evidently, therefore, those regions which contain large concentrations of corporate headquarters and higher-order functions such as research and development will have different employment and occupational profiles from those regions which consist predominantly of BRANCH PLANTS whose headquarters are elsewhere . . . .

Since the giant business corporations have shown considerable spatial flexibility so far, it is unlikely that they will cease to do so in the future. As the geographical scale of such flexibility continues to increase, the assembly and routine operations recently located in the peripheral areas of the US, the UK and other countries may well be relocated outside these countries altogether . . . the changing geography of employment cannot be isolated from developments at the global scale.

In order that this connection between the global scale of economic trends and events in particular locations is underlined, let us briefly examine two specific examples of corporate organisation.

2.5 Industrial linkages in the North West and North East

The North West

In Table 2.1, we can see outlined the industrial connections of the largest 54 firms active in the North West of England. These companies include all those employing in excess of 2,500 *manual* workers: between them, they account for 46 per cent of the region's manual workers (which emphasises, of course, why we have spent so long considering such large firms; in fact, the top 13 firms alone account for one quarter of the workforce in the area).

Table 2.1   The distribution of headquarters for the top 54 firms in the North West of England: ranks based on employment

Firm	Headquarters location	Rank	Main activities
Foreign Multinationals			
General Motors Corporation	Minneapolis USA	4	Automobiles
Ford Motor Co	Dearborn USA	10	Automobiles
Philips Glocilampen Fabricken	Holland	13	Electrical
Heinz, H. J., and Co.	Pittsburgh USA	46	Food
UK Multinationals/Nationals			
Controlled external to the region			
Imperial Chemical Industries	London	1	Chemicals/textiles
Courtaulds Ltd.	London	2	Textiles
GEC Ltd.	London	3	Electrical engineering
Unilever Ltd.	London	6	Food, detergents
British Insulated Callender Cables	London	7	Cables
Vickers Ltd.	London	8	Engineering
Plessey Co. Ltd.	Ilford, Essex	9	Electronics
Hawker Siddeley Group Ltd.	London	12	Engineering
Dunlop Holdings Ltd.	London	19	Rubber
Shell Transport and Trading Co.	London	21	Oil, petrochemicals
Lucas Industries Ltd.	Birmingham	22	Vehicles and aircraft parts
Reed International Ltd.	London	24	Paper, packaging
Stone Platt Industries Ltd.	London	25	Textile engineering
Tube Investments Ltd.	Birmingham	26	Engineering
British Aircraft Corporation	Weybridge, Surrey	27	Aerospace
Metal Box Ltd.	Reading	29	Packaging

Firm	Headquarters location	Rank	Main activities
Bowater Corporation Ltd.	London	30	Paper
Witington Investments (Ass. British Foods)	London	31	Food
Associated Biscuit Manufacturers	Reading	32	Food
Thorn Electrical Industries	London	33	Electrical
Imperial Group Ltd.	London	36	Tobacco
Distillers Co. Ltd.	Edinburgh	37	Whisky
Guest, Keen & Nettlefolds Ltd.	Smethwick, West Midlands	39	Engineering
Rank Hovis MacDougall	London	40	Food
BTR Ltd.	London	41	Rubber
United Biscuits (Holdings) Ltd.	Isleworth, Middx.	42	Food
Smith & Nephew Associated Co.'s Ltd.	London	43	Textiles, pharmaceuticals
Cadbury-Schweppes Ltd	London	45	Confectionary
Delta Metals Co. Ltd.	London	48	Electrical
Chloride Group Ltd.	London	49	Batteries
Bridon Ltd.	Doncaster	50	Wire, fibres, plastics
Glaxo Ltd.	London	53	Pharmaceuticals
Spirella Group Ltd.	Letchworth, Herts	54	Textiles
Locally controlled			
Pilkington Bros.	St Helens, Merseyside	11	Glass
Turner & Newall Ltd.	Manchester	14	Asbestos
Tootal Ltd.	Manchester	16	Textiles
Ferranti Ltd.	Oldham	17	Electrical engineering
Ward & Goldstone Ltd.	Salford	23	Cables, electrical
Cammell Laird Shipbuilders Ltd.	Birkenhead	28	Shipbuilding
Co-operative Wholesale Soc.	Manchester	36	Food
Renold Ltd.	Manchester	38	Power transmission
Rolls Royce Motor Holdings	Crewe	44	Transport engineering
Scapa Group Ltd.	Blackburn	47	Paper machinery
Vantona Ltd.	Bolton	51	Textiles
Mather & Platt	Manchester	52	Engineering
UK Public sector			
British Leyland	London	5	Trucks, cars
Ministry of Defence	London	15	Armaments
British Rail	London	18	Rail engineering
United Kingdom Atomic Energy Authority	London	20	Nuclear fuels
British Steel Corporation	London	34	Steel

Adapted from Lloyd and Reeve, 1982

1. Examine table 2.1. There are four groups of firms included; what are the differences between them?

2. Transfer the data to figure 2.6. Locate the ten largest firms; where are their headquarters?

3. Search the graph once more, and locate the ten smallest firms;

4. Reexamine the two categories and contrast the types of economic activity that the firms are involved in. Are there significant differences?

Discussion

The corporate structure of the North West tells us a great deal about the economic activity of the region. First, we can see that only 12 firms are firmly based in the area, and they are not amongst the largest on the list: indeed four are amongst the bottom eleven. The top ten are all controlled outside the region, and indeed two of these are managed in the USA.

Immediately then, we can identify the degree of external control. We can go further, however. We can see, for instance, that amongst the indigenous firms, several represent sectors which are declining more quickly than the average, such as shipbuilding and textiles (see ranks 16,28,51). This means that even firms with some history in the region will have to make dificult economic decisions in order to survive; Tootal, for example, has cut back its involvement in the UK to the tune of 7,100 jobs, whilst at the same time creating 14,000 jobs overseas. Nor are the other sectors inviolate. Since the collation of the table in 1977, Mather and Platt have been annexed by an Australian corporation, and British Leyland has closed down its plant in Speke, Liverpool.

The North East

In order to contrast the above study of headquarters with a brief account of a branch plant, we turn to the North East. There, Findus has recently announced the establishment of a new frozen food plant, which will produce pizzas. Several aspects of the development are of interest to us here:

1. The plant cost £30 million, of which 22 per cent will come from regional aid in the form of grants for building and plant.

2. The plant employs 50 management/clerical staff; 40 skilled operatives and 450 'process operatives': 300 of these are part-time employees.

3. All employees receive lectures on the company's history and all receive identical benefits and eat in the same canteen.

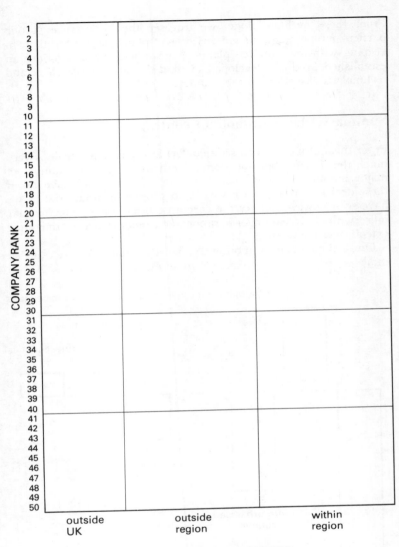

Figure 2.6   *Company ranks- and headquarters' location*

> *Use the data in table 2.1 to complete the graph. It may be useful in addition to mark whether you think the firms are in growing or declining sectors. Publications like the* Financial Times *can give an indication of how companies and types of industries are prospering.*

From these outlines alone, we can see the importance of one particular type of labour for this type of plant. Notice too that, in keeping with most branch plants, this site will simply produce an established product, developed by skilled market researchers and technicians elsewhere in the country.

2.6 Summary: the metropolitan context

From this outline, we can see that ED at the regional scale is very much dependent upon locational decisions taken by a number of major manufacturers. Once, these same firms would have taken these decisions based upon very rigid geographical criteria; as we have seen however, today the corporate interface is concerned far more with the creation of a rational business structure that may extend over continents.

One last comment is in order. As figure 2.7 indicates, we can also think of manufacturing changes in terms of *urban* issues. As we

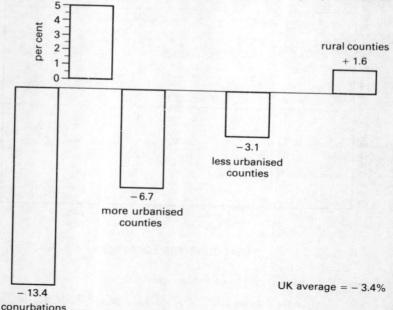

Average % manufacturing employment change 1971–6 by groups of counties

per cent

rural counties
+ 1.6

− 3.1
less urbanised
counties

− 6.7
more urbanised
counties

− 13.4
conurbations

UK average = − 3.4%

Figure 2.7   Employment change in manufacturing industry classified in terms of urbanisation within different counties (from Keeble, 1981)

know from book 3, large metropolitian centres are steadily losing population, and are unattractive also to firms. This means that in part, ED in regions is connected with metropolitan decline in centres like Newcastle, Glasgow, Manchester and Liverpool, or the relative attractiveness of smaller centres like Norwich or Swansea.

This reminds us again of the extent to which ED is inter-related at different scales: the global, the regional, and now it seems, the urban as well. Let us examine this aspect in greater detail.

Key issues

TECHNOLOGICAL CHANGE AND JOB LOSS The industrial process depends upon making goods as cheaply as possible: without high returns, industries cannot attract investors or continue to reinvest in new products. There are two ways to maintain levels of profitability: one is to change the process of production, the other is to reduce expenditure upon labour. These two issues are not necessarily related. British industry could have changed (i.e. updated) its production processes in the 1960s when demand was high. It failed to do this, and left the changes until the present. What we are seeing at present is a long-delayed process of technological change being in part financed by enforced labour redundancy. The technical change is varied; it can be as simple as speeding up the production line, through to installing 'robots'.

BRANCH PLANT A branch plant is any factory unit which is controlled from outside the immediate area. Thus in the North East for example, approximately 75 per cent of industrial units are ultimately controlled/owned by firms based in other regions. One outcome of this external control is that it is very easy for large firms to close their remote operations in times of loss or product change.

SUN-BELT Many commentators have identified the growth of the sun-belt in the USA. It is a broad zone, stretching across the southern half of the continent. It would be a mistake to pay too much attention to the implications of the name. It is not simply that economic growth is occurring here because of a superior climate (indeed, in some contexts, that would be difficult to argue: Florida in summer for example is extremely unpleasant). Rather, we are seeing ED taking place in new areas, where costs are low, where labour is available and where planning controls are minimal. In 1981 in consequence, 15 per cent of all building permits granted in the US were in Texas – and 9 per cent of the national total was granted in Houston, which has no planning controls whatsoever.

INDUSTRIAL INERTIA It should not be assumed that all industrial investment is highly mobile, however. *Infrastructure*: buildings, machinery, link roads and so on are expensive, and thus firms may hold on to these sites, or sell them to growing firms which can thus expend very cheaply. In this way, patterns of change may be delayed by many years.

3
The organisation of urban space

.1 Location and accessibility

We have already discussed the evolution of the city in book 4, paying particular attention to the relationship between the historical core and the later peripheral developments. Of course, this is not the only way of analysing the city, in so far as individual users of urban space are making locational decisions on a day-to-day basis too. Thus, for example, the continued existence of the Central Business District is not only a function of historical factors, but the outcome of contemporary choices as well.

There are several models which have been developed by geographers and economists which attempt to explain these locational decisions. Of these, the best known is that produced by William Alonso, an urban economist. His basic approach is to emphasise the importance of *accessibility*; that is, he argues that land-uses in the city are determined by the user's willingness to pay for the most accessible sites. In turn, because the city is usually thought of as a circular phenomenon, it follows that the most desirable location will be somewhere in the centre, as this is the point of maximum accessibility. (You should sketch a circular city, and attempt to demonstrate this point for yourself.)

Urban land-uses can thus be seen to take shape in the way outlined in figure 3.1. Let us concentrate upon the top graph, figure 3.1(a). There we have two axes; one relates to distance from the central city, the other relates to a user's willingness to pay for a site. This willingness is called a BID-RENT. The bid-rent offered by a commercial user is shown to be quite steep: the user (perhaps a retail store) will pay a good deal to be near the centre, as this will guarantee a high turnover of customers, and a great deal less to be even a small distance away.

Let us now introduce an industrial user. He or she is not prepared to bid quite as highly, although a central location is still desirable (perhaps for agglomeration purposes). From the graph, we can see that commerce outbids industry at the centre, which thus explains the CBD. Similarly, industry outbids residential developers, who are aiming to buy land for new home construction.

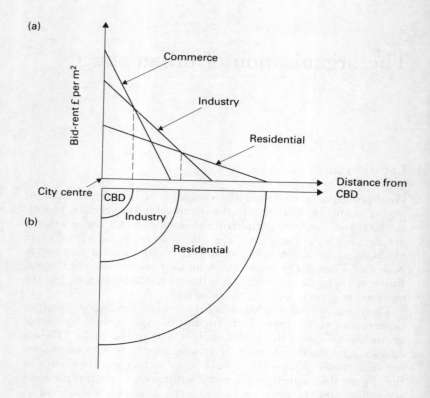

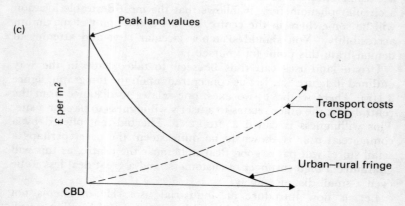

Figure 3.1 (a) bid-rents from competing land-uses;
(b) the pattern of land-uses resulting from the bid-rents in (a);
(c) the land values resulting from the land-uses and bid-rents in
(a) and (b).

Workers want to live near to shops and their work, but cannot afford to bid highly. Thus again, industry outbids the developer.

Examining figure 3.1(a) once more, we can see therefore that commerce outbids industry, which in turn outbids residential users, as we move further away from the CBD. We can display this in simple map terms in the following way: first, drop a perpendicular line from the point at which the bid-rents coincide(dotted lines); then, assume that the graph is turned through 90°, or one quadrant of our circular city. This will reveal the land-use pattern shown in figure 3.1(b), which can, of course, be extended for the whole city.

.2 A case-study of urban land-use development

Alonso's model assumes that the process of ED taking place in urban areas is not constrained by the legacy of past development: in other words, that new land-uses are not determined by what has gone before. It is often difficult to find examples where this assumption can be investigated, although one good study is provided by an examination of what occurred in San Francisco, California following the earthquake of 1906. More than half the housing and two thirds of the job sites were destroyed by the earthquake or the subsequent fire, and free evacuation was offered to residents in the hope of easing the homelessness: 300,000 left the city, and at least 70,000 never returned.

In the immediate disaster period, we see the process of ED in action without constraint. As Haas, Kates and Bowden (1977, p. 75) have shown, there was an ordered period of reconstruction.

> (In) any large disaster, some dislocation is inevitable. A chain reaction of relocation, displacement and further relocation is initiated by commercial and industrial activities and residents able to pay the highest rents . . .. The most significant locational decision in the rebuilding of San Francisco was made by a major bank four months after the earthquake; other banks, by their decisions and acts of rebuilding, defined the extent of the district in the first year. Large financial institutions – the exchanges, insurance companies and later the leading real estate concerns – followed quickly in sequence, establishing distinct stockbroking, insurance, real estate and banking foci within the new financial district. Medium-sized and smaller establishments then fleshed out the larger financial district and its constituent sub-districts, a process lasting three years.

This process is illustrated neatly in figure 3.2, which shows the way in which the activities able to offer the highest bid-rents (i.e. those with the greatest 'centrality') were the ones who relocated first;

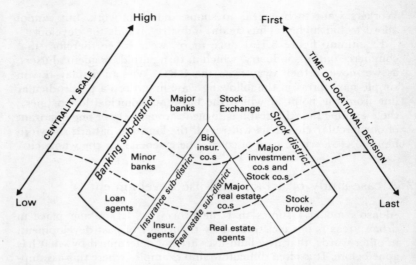

Figure 3.2   The sequence of return within the financial district, San Francisco, 1906–09 (from Haas et al., 1977)

their less affluent counterparts had to wait to then complete their locational decision.

Once the financial district had begun its consolidation, other land-uses were able to make their locational decisions. A new retailing ('apparel') district appeared, as did a hotel sector; both had been displaced by the new, enlarged finance sector. The larger process of reordering is summarised in figure 3.3, which shows the ultimate geographical outcome of ED in the post-earthquake period. As we can see there is a close correlation between the ability of a land-user to bid for a site, and the speed with which return occurred.

Of interest too is the fact that the new economic landscape within the city displaced entirely some uses (Haas, Kates and Bowden, 1977, p. 1978).

The extended delays attending re-establishment by activities formerly located near the edge of the central business district and the diseconomies suffered by activities forced to take suboptimal locations for up to eight years, frequently caused failure of those activities or their relocation beyond the bounds of the disaster-stricken city. There were for example, 450 manufacturing jobs fewer in San Francisco three years after the disaster than there were before it . . . . Other losers are the wholesale and manufacturing concerns dependent upon low rents of old loft buildings in near-central locations, close to the external economies that

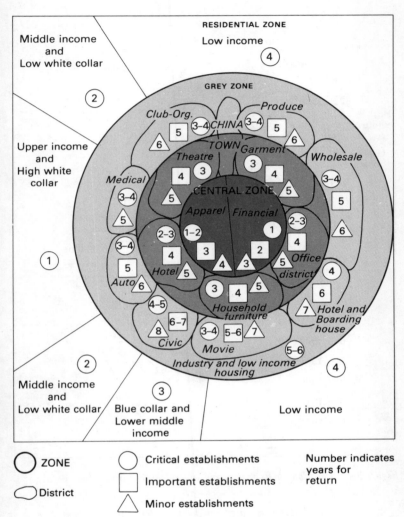

Figure 3.3   Temporal and spatial sequence of return, San Francisco following the 1906 earthquake and fire (from Haas et al., 1977)

come from the concentration of hundreds of linked activities in a tightly circumscribed area.

As we can see from figure 3.3, the residential areas were amongst the slowest to relocate and become re-established. Again, cues were taken from those able to bid the highest, with the net result that

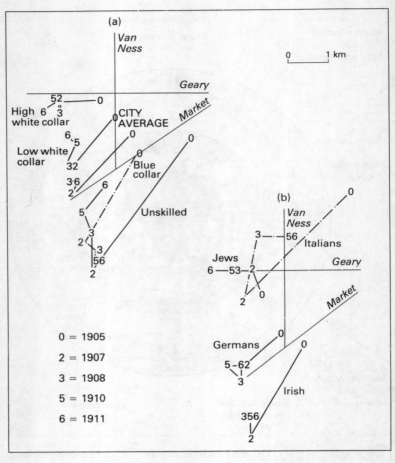

Figure 3.4 Location shifts in housing concentration (from Haas et al., 1977)

> The diagram is based around the intersecting streets in San Francisco of Van Ness, Geary and Market. For the years 1905–11, the researchers have identified the centres of different ethnic communities and different income groups. They have then plotted how these groups shifted after the earthquake in 1906. From the first-time period (1 year after the earthquake) through to 1911 (period 6), we can see how the groups were displaced and then attempted to relocate their homes. For example, we can see that the Italian group was heavily displaced, but slowly moved back towards the original neighbourhoods.

another locational displacement occurred: this is summarised in figure 3.4.

> At one end of the spectrum, upper-class districts and individuals stabilised rapidly, whereas unskilled workers were still in motion five years after the disaster. The sequence of return placed greatest stress on the social class and economic activities lowest in the ranking of activities. They were dislocated for the longest period, and forced finally to locate on land unclaimed by activities above them in the ranking, to suburbanise to other East Bay towns, or to leave the Bay Area altogether. . . . Much of the new housing was built in the West. The very steep rent gradient ensured that only the rich could bid for housing in this district, in the straightened financial circumstances of the post-disaster period. As a result, the west became an upper-class sector with an exclusiveness hitherto unknown in San Francisco.

As figure 3.4 indicates, the occupation of the western hills by the most affluent produced a major displacement for all social groups, away from the old residential core around the intersection of Van Ness and Geary (streets). The biggest shift was experienced by the unskilled/Irish residents, who were displaced for some distance, and only re-entered some residential districts in 1910–11.

3 A resumé of the economic approach

The painstaking historical recreation undertaken by Hass and his colleagues indicates quite clearly that what was in effect a new city was created in San Francisco post-1906, and that its geographic organisation resulted from the way in which different land-users bid for particular locations; overall, the basic tenets of the Alonsian model seem to be justified.

However, we must be clear about the applicability of the model to other time periods and other cultural contexts.

1. Reexamine the assumptions of the Alonsian approach. Compare these with what you know about the following within the contemporary British city:
   (a) the trends in the location of retailing;
   (b) the trends in the location of many types of industry;
   (c) the nature of the housing market and residential location patterns.

2. The model focuses upon *land*. What decision-makers in the city though actually purchase land, rather than take over existing buildings?

Discussion

The accessibility model that we have looked at above is excellent for examining the early twentieth-century city, in which movement was fairly closely constrained (see, for instance, chapter 3, book 4). It is however becoming less and less useful as a basis for understanding present trends. The heightened mobility provided by the increased ownership of motor vehicles has meant that the process of ED within cities is not restricted to traditional sites. Thus, for instance, it is now possible to build shopping centres on the margins of cities, with the expectation that consumers will travel out of town to use them; in this way, consumers enjoy ease of parking, whilst retailers can build larger stores on cheap, peripheral sites, thus increasing their profits. Although only 10 such stores were built in Britain in the 1960s, 106 were built between 1976 and 1979 alone.

Similarly, industry is less constrained to operate in the inner city than has previously been the case – indeed, many firms use the ending of a lease as a good incentive to get away from escalating rents, narrow streets which make deliveries and collections of goods very difficult, and the varied stresses and strains which contribute to urban existence. Once again, out-of-town sites provide the attractions of lower rents and thus higher margins of return.

The housing question is rather more complicated, and introduces the issue of land. Alonso emphasised that his model dealt with *land*-use, despite that fact that nearly all users of urban space purchase or rent existing *buildings*. However, as soon as we start discussing particular parts of the HOUSING MARKET, we come up against various controls which interfere with the highly rational outline that he proposed. The most obvious example here is the case of local authority housing, which as we have seen accounts for approximately one third of all households in the UK. However, public housing has very specific entry qualifications, and very varied types of dwelling. For complicated historical reasons, which often relate to the patterns of slum clearance and urban renewal, many blocks of council flats have been built on what should be expensive land near to the CBD. The net result of this is that many low-income families can be found in locations that do not in any way fit in with the bid-rent predictions.

A second problem that emerges here is uncovered if we focus upon house prices (as opposed to land costs). As we have seen, *land* costs are assumed to *fall* with distance from the point of maximum accessibility (check again figure 3.1(c)). However, most studies of *house* prices indicate that they *rise* as one moves further from the central city. It is this aspect that poses the biggest problem for an understanding of ED using any kind of economic model.

4 An alternative model of residential land-use

Another examination of figure 3.1 will underline that Alonso's model does not help us to understand residential location if we accept that house prices rise away from the CBD. As figure 3.1(c) emphasises, an economic interpretation is possible if we contrast falling land values and rising transport costs; in other words, one expenditure can be offset against the other. This is obviously not possible if we contrast house prices (which rise away from the CBD) and transport costs (which also rise).

One attempt to explain the residential location decision is outlined in figure 3.5. This model focuses upon the importance of

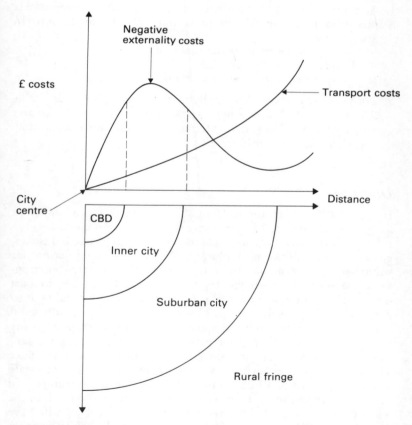

Figure 3.5   *The distribution of negative externality costs in the urban area, their relation to transport costs, and the outcome in terms of land-uses*

externalities in determining house prices. We discussed externalities in book 2, where we emphasised the importance of positive externalities (schools, recreation facilities etc.) and negative externalities (noisy roads, rubbish tips) in determining the quality of life for different neighbourhoods. The model proposes that there is a predictable distribution of these externalities within the city, and that negative externality costs are highest in the inner city, and then lower as one moves further from the CBD. With this pattern, it is once again possible to produce an economic model of ED, in so far as we can assume that consumers will either live close to the CBD (poor environment but low transport costs) or in the suburbs (good environment but higher transport costs).

1. Attempt to explain the distribution of negative externalities predicted in figure 3.5; in particular you should attempt to account for:
   (*a*) high negative costs in the inner city;
   (*b*) lower costs in the suburbs;
   (*c*) an increase in costs in the urban – rural fringe.

2. For your own urban area, apply the model to reality. Using table 2.1 from book 2 as a guide, assess whether there is a greater concentration of negative externalities in the inner areas than elsewhere in the built-up area.

Discussion

In most urban areas, the residential environment has a consistent geographical pattern. The inner city is a poor environment because it has – historically – the least-planned mix of things like industries, gasworks and decaying buildings. Conversely, one reason for suburban expansion has been the attractive residential environment on offer; in consequence, the process of ED has in part depended upon the low rates of externality costs, enhanced by low-density housing developments. This environment is generally good therefore, until one reaches the urban fringe, at which point many essential services (shops, recreation, sometimes even sewerage) become less easy to obtain. As figure 3.6 indicates, the importance of externalities is explicitly revealed by an examination of estate agent prospectuses, which consistently mention these features. In specific localities, other types of features will be emphasised; in the vicinity of an airport, for example, prospective clients will have their attention drawn to the location of flight paths, whilst in other towns it is often desirable to live in the catchments of particular schools, which are believed to have the best academic records or the least likelihood of closure.

Sworders

Established 1782

House and Estate Agents
Auctioneers Valuers
Surveyors
Insurance Agents

G.E.Sworder & Sons

18 Adams House,
Post Office Walk,
The High,
Harlow,
Essex CM20 1BD.
Tel: (0279) 21511.

A CHARMING PERIOD COTTAGE IN THE HEART OF THIS
MOST SOUGHT AFTER VILLAGE

Situated in this very popular village which offers
various amenities including local shops, schools and
a bus service to all surrounding areas. Harlow Town
Centre is only four miles from Hunsdon and offers an
excellent multiple shopping centre plus many
recreational facilities.

 **Mullucks and company**

Surveyors, Estate Agents, Valuers.
4 Westgate, The High, Harlow, Essex. CM20 1JW
Tel: (0279) 443311

Also at Bishop's Stortford (0279) 55074. Saffron Walden (0799) 21462, Gt Dunmow (0371) 2046
A.J. Mullucks FRICS CAAV. D.R. Burch M.A. Sumpster ARICS G.R.E. Wakelin ARICS
Local Manager D. Masters

A SPACIOUS FULLY DETACHED PROPERTY ON SECLUDED
CORNER PLOT

Convenient for all amenities and facing a small green.
Harlow main line station (30 minutes to City), the
Town Centre, hospital, churches, schools, Harlow
sports centre and golf course are all within about
10 minutes walk.

*Figure 3.6   Examples of estate agents prospectuses emphasising the
importance of externalities in the locational decision*

3.5   Constraints within the housing market

The mention of phenomena like school catchments reminds us that the residential location decision is subject to many constraints. The desire to live in a particular catchment area may be a self-imposed restriction upon choice, but we have already examined other examples of real constraint. In book 4, for instance, we noted that building societies will only rarely grant mortgages in the inner city. Similarly, large tracts of local authority housing 'interfere' with the simple model proposed in figure 3.5, because to many home-owners, council tenants are not seen as a positive externality.

What all this implies is that a simple model which tries to reduce ED within the city to an issue like accessibility is doomed to failure. When we look at just the residential context, we find the city to be a patchwork quilt of inner city housing, council housing and owner-occupation: this is revealed for the city of Newcastle-upon-Tyne in figure 3.7. Each of these housing spaces (notably the more recent ones), has been developed as a result of a highly complex series of decisions taken by residential developers, local planners and, of course, residents.

These housing spaces tell us a great deal about the process of ED within the city. Residential developers build homes on the basis that the most desirable (and thus the most profitable) are those which have the best facilities in terms of services, and the greatest exclusivity. Residents too have a role to play here, in that they work very hard to maintain this exclusivity. An example recounted by geographer Brian Robson indicates this. He examines relations between two housing estates, which are shown in figure 3.8. When the private estate was built in 1938, a barrier of open space was left, in order to insulate it from the council estate to the north. When in 1970 plans were drawn up to upgrade the road connecting the public housing estate with Moor Road, it was also proposed that the traffic from the council area should be re-routed through Bodley Avenue, a private road.

As Robson argues, the plans were seen as a direct threat to some residents' exclusivity, and they responded by first attempting legal, then political action; when this failed, they resorted to the practical expedient of building physical barricades across Bodley Avenue (see figure 3.8). Their actions, although illegal, ultimately delayed the proposed road for some ten years. Robson states (1982, pp. 45–46) that:

> the local residential environment provides the most common locus of conflict within the city not simply because residential areas comprise the largest single land-use, but because of the strong commitment that people have to the immediate area in

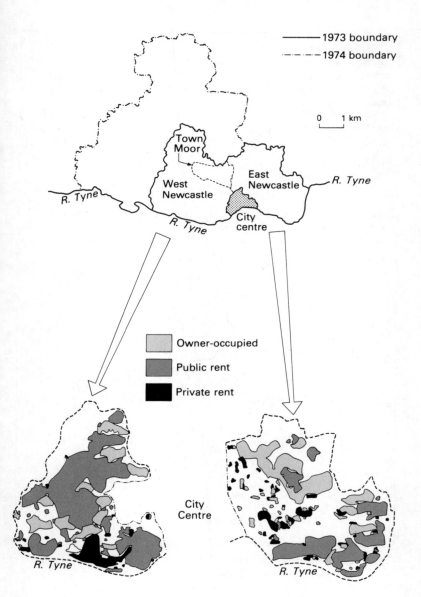

Figure 3.7   The distribution of housing spaces in Newcastle-upon-Tyne

> *Each housing space consists of similar types of dwelling: council housing, privately-owned housing and flats rented from private landlords. The data were collected from rate books held by the Local Authority.*

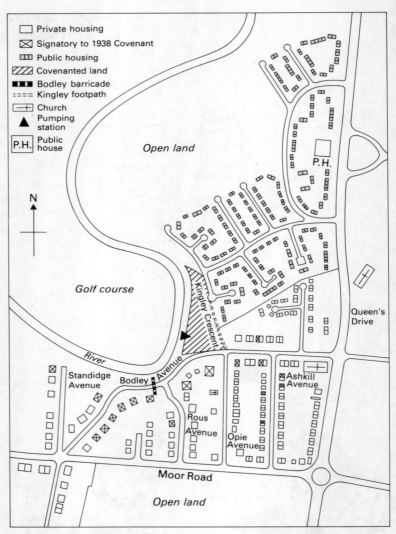

Figure 3.8   The setting for conflicts between owners and renters: see text
for details (from Robson, 1982)

which they live, a commitment which is reinforced in the case
of the owner-occupier by a very direct financial vested interest.
No less than in medieval times, the present day English castle
is apt to be defended . . . .

What prompts residential conflict is almost invariably a concern with minimising the negative externalities which are represented by the real or perceived threats of land-use or social changes in an area and with maximising the converse positive externalities. We can think of three general categories into which such externalities might fall. The physical environment includes such physical elements as parks and open spaces, or such negative externalities as heavier road traffic, increased air pollution or noise. The resource environment includes the benefits of good schools, shops, cultural and recreational facilities . . . and welfare facitities such as clinics. The social environment represents an externality less readily specified, but none the less important since 'compatible' neighbours help to ensure that life-styles do not jar and that there is common ground for any collaborative search for the tangible positive externalities and a common front in resisting the negative.

3.6 Summary

In this chapter, we have again taken a simple path. We began by investigating the process of ED within cities, by suggesting that the locational decision is based – as usual – upon the need to maximise financial returns, and that these returns are governed by the need to find highly accessible sites. However, as we also pointed out, access is far less important in the contemporary urban scene. Central city functions are keen to leave, and residential land-use can only be understood in terms of highly complex motivations.

The accessibility model is of course an old one; indeed its antecedents go back a century and a half to original studies of *rural* land-uses. Let us now examine these, and ascertain whether their applicability has also been diminished.

Key issues

BID-RENT The bid-rent curve measures an individual's willingness to occupy a particular location. Thus close to the CBD, the bid-rent will be high, as this is a desirable location; further away the bid-rent will be lower, which reflects the fact that it is a less attractive site, and therefore that the bidder is prepared to offer only a smaller sum.

HOUSING MARKET We have already discussed the structure of the British housing market in book 4. We showed the way in which a single market is now split into three parts: the owner-occupied sector, the council housing sector, and the private rental market. One of the key issues within the housing market is the way in which each sector has distinct geographical overtones. Thus private renting is associated with the inner city, and owner-occupation was historically connected with the growth of suburbs (again, see book 4). One of the aspects of housing identified by many sociologists is the way in which owners and renters can be very antagonistic, to the extent that local political rows can develop between them. In book 1, for instance, we showed a picture of the Cutteslowe Wall, which was built by owners because they did not want nearby council tenants entering their neighbourhood. These tensions are a result of different outlooks, perceptions, styles of life and class differences.

CITIES AS EXAMPLES OF ECONOMIC DEVELOPMENT In this chapter we have emphasised the issue of ED *within* cities. We should not overlook, however, the argument that cities are themselves aspects of ED. As we showed in book 4, the rapid growth of the city in the 1920s and 1930s was very much an economic issue, in so far as investors saw bricks and mortar as a safer form of investment than shares or bonds. The development of most settlements is a complicated question, but there are various examples of cities which have been built solely as speculative investments: places such as Orlando or Clearwater in Florida, which depend upon retirement or vacation residents, are good examples.

4
The organisation of rural land-uses

4.1 The farming fathers

Although Alonso's model of urban land-use may appear relatively sophisticated, we can see echoes of that approach in a study undertaken as early as 1826, by another German, Heinrich von Thünen. The latter was an affluent landowner, who examined his financial records and attempted to make some theoretical sense of them. He argued that agricultural land-use was determined by a notion that he called ECONOMIC RENT. Different crops or land-uses were grown most profitably in specific locations, which could be summarised hypothetically as in figure 4.1. He called his model landscape 'an isolated state', in order to indicate that it was an abstraction of reality, rather than a universal prediction. As we can see, von Thünen predicted a series of concentric zones around an urban area, which acted as the sole market. In close proximity to the market, he predicted market gardening and dairying, and then a zone of timber (still important for fuel in urban areas at that time). Further from the market, he suggests zones of arable production, and ultimately cattle production. As we can also see, the pattern is distorted where alternative transportation modes exist, and where another market is available.

Von Thünen's concept of economic rent is not greatly different from the notion of a bid-rent, and makes the same assumptions about the importance of accessibility. The mechanism is outlined in figure 4.2. In the first diagram, we take into account the market price of the crop at the point of purchase. The farmer has to take into account the costs of transporting the crop to market, which obviously increases with distance from the urban centre. In consequence, the economic returns from a unit of land will fall in step with its distance from the market. Of course, this can also be affected by the intensive or extensive manner in which the crop is grown (figure 4.2(b)); a crop that is extensive i.e. does not involve large inputs of labour or capital, will produce greater returns out on the margins, where high transport costs have already wiped out the profitability of other activities. Consequently, when we put these two factors together, we find the now-familiar pattern of intersect-

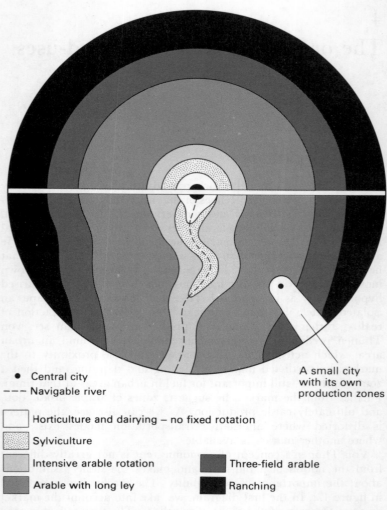

Figure 4.1   Von Thünen's system of land-use: his 'isolated state'

> *Note that the model assumes equal transport costs in all directions, except where shown (a river); a single market, and uniform fertility.*

ing rent curves, which can be manipulated to give zones of land-use: figure 4.2(c).

Once again, we can also express these inter-relationships algebraically, using the following formula:

$$ER = Ym - (Yc + Yt) \qquad (2)$$

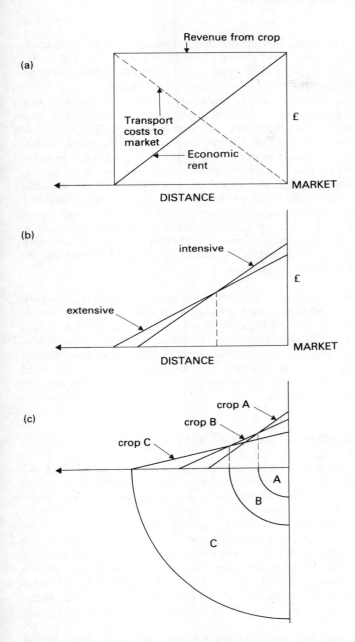

Figure 4.2 (a) *The relationship between transport cost and economic rent;*
(b) *between intensive and extensive crops;*
(c) *economic rents and patterns of land-use.*

In formal language, this means that we can predict the economic rent by relating the yield per unit of land (Y) to the costs of transport (t) and the costs of cultivation (c); these must then be subtracted from the market price (m).

When we examine von Thünen's predictions once more, we can see that different land-uses have a geographical distribution as a result of both production costs and transport costs. Thus the first zone of market garden production involves high inputs of capital and labour, but can command high prices at market; (the question of perishability also dictates proximity to market: as we showed in book 4, dairy production was a feature of *urban* land-use until the end of the nineteenth century). In contrast, silviculture (or forestry) involves few inputs of labour or capital, but necessitates high transport costs; in consequence, a close relationship to the market is involved. Beyond these zones are varying degrees of intensive arable production, and at the spatial margins, highly *extensive* activities are the only ones possible.

Note: the term *margin* is used, particularly by economists, in a very specific way. Marginal land is thus a unit that is only just profitable, once the costs of bringing it into production are taken into consideration. In this discussion, however, we have followed von Thünen in reducing the importance of fertility, and emphasising the importance of spatial factors. Consequently, the notions of marginal land and spatial margins (the edges of cultivation) are taken to be synonomous.

4.2 An application of the von Thünen model

To what extent are the assumptions of this model of ED in rural areas applicable to an understanding of the real world? As we shall see below, it is difficult today to find examples of close inter-relationships between town and country in the way that von Thünen envisaged. It is possible, however, to examine in a general way the principles that underlie the model; in other words, we can investigate the *processes* that are discussed rather than the *patterns*.

Our example is taken from the developing frontier in eighteenth-century North America; as we can see in figure 4.3, the rural hinterland was economically developed in part to supply the urbanising seaboard on the east coast (see chapter 4, book 3). The principles of economic rent propounded by von Thünen work well in explaining the margins of cultivation that grew up in the 1750s; as we can see in the first graph, zones of dairying, silviculture, horticulture, arable production and ranching existed as predicted. Of additional interest though is the added zone of liquor production

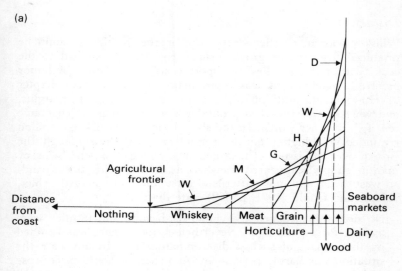

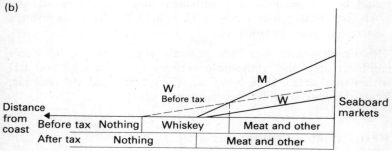

Figure 4.3 An economic interpretation of the 1794 Whiskey rebellion (from Abler et al., 1971)

which emerged beyond the ranching zone. This existed until 1794, when the emerging national government placed an excise tax on spirits. As we can see from the second graph, this altered the profitability of liquor production, its economic rent fell, and in consequence the 'agricultural frontier' was cut short, with the result that a rebellion broke out.

1. Explain why an additional zone of production emerged beyond the area of ranching;

2. Why did the distillation of whiskey prove unrealistic once it was taxed?

3. What ultimately happened to whiskey production?

Discussion

Whiskey was an excellent 'crop' out on the frontier: it could be produced from grains grown extensively, and dispatched to the coast with relatively low transport costs, as a bottle of liquor involves a major weight loss in production (unlike beer: see chapter 2). However, the addition of the excise tax cut into profit margins, and whiskey was then less profitable than ranching: its economic rent fell, in other words. In the short term, the Whiskey rebellion reminded Washington that the frontiersman had already fought the British over the issues of taxation; in the long term, the 'whiskey margin' simply reappeared elsewhere as the whole frontier expanded westwards, and new patterns of economic rent emerged. Abler, Adams and Gould (1971, p. 362) state that:

> No doubt the rugged individualists beyond the frontier were looking for a good fight. Nevertheless, their anger was justified by the impact of such a discriminatory tax. In any case the situation was hardly permanent. As urban seaboard prices rose and better transport and settlement advanced westward, the whiskey frontier moved also, and western Pennsylvania farmers turned to other pursuits.

This example underlines the general veracity of von Thünen's emphasis upon the relationship between economic rent and ED within rural areas. It is, however, self-evidently a dated example; let us therefore consider modern conditions.

4.3 Restrictions and limitations

In analysing von Thünen's work, we have briefly outlined several of his assumptions. Examine these with a view to determining how realistic they are in a contemporary context:

1. *the isolated state*: the relationship between town (market) and countryside (producer);

2. *transport costs*: the importance of movement costs in restricting mobility of goods;

3. *intensive/extensive production*: the assumption of uniform fertility.

Discussion

Von Thünen's model is an idealisation, and therefore assumptions about transportation being uniform (in terms of increases with distance in all directions) and no variations in fertility are to be expected. However, we need to question to what extent these assumptions can still be made in terms of changes within agricultural practice over the last century.

With respect to fertility, we can reasonably argue that it is now *more* possible to assume that fertility can be ignored than ever before. The widespread availability of fertilisers means that *for those who can afford them*, large variations in fertility are unlikely, (this will not of course apply in developing countries, due to the cost factor).

Second, and more problematically, we can no longer assume that rural areas supply one market. As we shall see below, the agricultural market is extremely complex.

Third, major changes have also occurred with respect to transportation. The real costs of movement have fallen dramatically decade by decade, and technological changes such as refrigeration have made the shipping of perishable foodstuffs relatively easy. This point is made in table 4.1, which shows the way in which London's food imports have widened geographically, to encompass world markets.

Leaving aside the question of fertility, we can see that the isolated state no longer exists. It is relatively easy to ship goods to wherever the best prices are being paid: conversely, consumers in one town can buy from wherever prices are lowest. This means that ED in rural areas is no longer a simple relation – town and country – but a very complicated process. When farmers in Rutland are competing with producers throughout the world, and shipping their produce to many consumers, it is difficult for them to know what are the most profitable crops.

Table 4.1   *The increase in average distances over which agricultural produce travelled to London markets between 1831–1913 (in kms)*

Imports	1831–35	1856–60	1871–75	1891–95	1901–13
Fruit and vegetables	0	518	535	1,140	3,008
Live animals	0	1,008	1,392	5,648	7,200
Butter, cheese eggs, etc.	419	848	2,144	2,576	4,992
Feed grains	1,376	3,248	3,888	5,184	7,728
Flax and seeds	3,432	5,200	4,432	6,528	6,240
Meat and tallow	3,200	4,640	5,984	8,080	10,000
Wheat and flour	3,880	3,472	6,720	8,240	9,520
Wool and hides	3,680	14,128	16,000	17,616	17,440
Weighted average for all above imports	2,912	5,840	6,880	8,080	9,408

Source: Peet, 1969, p. 295

In a free, economic environment, like the one experienced by von Thünen and his contemporaries, such uncertainties would result in food shortages in some sectors and gluts in others. In consequence, farmers in a country like Britain are now cushioned by an extensive system of AGRICULTURAL SUPPORTS, both from the national government and the European Economic Community. These financial supports mean that individual farmers are less dependent upon factors like the weather and changes in market prices: it also means that farming overall is less of a risk, and more like any other business activity.

4.4 The changing countryside

Throughout developed societies, agriculture is in a state of change. Government intervention and the dependence upon chemical preparations to improve fertility have drawn farmers into the worlds of politics and economics. Perhaps more importantly, other interests have been drawn into the world of agriculture. Increased profits are attractive to businesses searching for new fields of investment – in this instance, quite literally.

This trend can be seen most markedly in the United States, where we can see the growth of so-called 'agribusiness'. This is most marked in the production of soy beans, which now proceeds simply as a business rather than the growing of a crop by individual farmers. When processed, the soy bean produces both soy oil and soy meal. The oil is used for the manufacture of margarine and cooking oil, whilst the meal can be processed in many different ways: by-products include animal feed, artificial meat, and synthetic dairy products. With the exception of the former, all soy products are very important in the preparation of 'institutional' food. There has thus been a temptation for soy producers to integrate their production in a vertical sense; it is common for one corporation to own farms, chemical processing plants (to separate the beans), and then a host of subsidiary companies which consume and reprocess the by-products: these include drug companies, poultry producers, and canning concerns. At the end of the integration process are even trucking companies to distribute the seemingly endless by-products and fast-food restaurants which consume the cooking oils and artificial meats that have been developed.

Such integration works best if all the activities are undertaken on a large scale. Central Soya Inc. operates 26 processing mills, but most interesting from our point of view is Tenneco (Tennessee Oil Pipeline Company), which now farms in excess of 1.4 *million* acres across five states. This means that ED in rural areas is increasingly part of very big business in America, and that land-use decisions are taken to fit in with very broad industrial considerations rather than local agricultural ones.

The situation in the UK is rather different, because the growth of agribusiness has come *after* the development of most of the profitable agricultural land; in consequence, it would be prohibitively expensive to buy up enormously large estates (although this does not mean that land is not an investment commodity: see below). In this country therefore, agribusiness has tended to deal direct with the larger and more efficient farmers. The relationship between the two is based upon both inputs and outputs. By inputs we mean the consumption by farmers of foodstuffs and various chemicals, and by outputs we mean the various agricultural products that are required by agribusinesses. Very often, firms will supply the former, and offset the costs against the latter, making it easier for the already efficient farm to consume ever-higher amounts of chemicals and thereby to increase productivity yet again. The scale of these inter-relationships is shown by sociologist Howard Newby (1982, p. 15):

> BOCM–Silcock is a subsidiary of the multinational combine Unilever, which also produces Bird's Eye frozen food, Vesta packaged meals, Batchelors tinned vegetables and soups, Walls ice cream and meat products, Blue Band, Stork, Summer County Flora and Echo margarine, Spry and Cookeen lard, Crisp'n'Dry cooking oil, and detergent and toilet preparations such as Lux, Persil etc . . . . Unilever also owns shipping lines, meat wholesalers and processors, paper mills, supermarkets and much, much more – 812 companies in 75 countries manufacturing over 1000 products. Unilever is the most spectacular example of the vertically-integrated multinational agribusiness corporation, but it is by no means unique in controlling a proportion of both agricultural inputs (feedstuffs) and outputs. Farmers find that when it comes to marketing their produce (a notoriously weak aspect of British agriculture) they are drawn into the embrace of the food processing industry, an industry which is also dominated by a few companies in most commodities.

As Newby and Utting imply, Unilever is only the most spectacular example of the genre, and the degrees of linkage enjoyed by other firms is shown in table 4.2.

1. We have seen in the American case that agribusinesses depend upon very large farms. What are the likely implications of this new agricultural revolution for British farming?

2. What are these changes likely to mean for rural ED and the resulting patterns of land-use?

Table 4.2 The degree of integration displayed by leading agribusinesses in the UK

	Agricultural production	Animal feeds	Wholesaling	Retailing
Unilever	x	x		x
ABF			x	x
CWS	x		x	x
Cavenham		x		x
RBM	x	x	x	x
Tate and Lyle	x			
Unigate	x			x
Union International	x		x	x
Cadbury-Schweppes	x			
Spillers	x	x	x	
Brooke Bond Liebig	x			
J. Lyons				x
Imperial Foods	x	x	x	x
Fitch Lovell	x		x	x
FMC	x		x	
United Biscuits				x
H. J. Heinz	x			
J. Bibby		x		
Booker McConnell	x		x	x

Source: Newby and Utting, 1982

Discussion

There are three main trends that we can detect at present in the countryside. The first of these is a consistent growth in the size of land holdings. Britain has historically always possessed large estates (the monarch is still a major landowner, for instance), but there is evidence that the average farm size is growing. This in part relates to rationalisation, and the buying up of adjacent units to make bigger farms (listeners to *The Archers* will be familiar with this activity). It is also a function of the continued demise of marginal (particularly upland) farms, which itself relates to the pressures of agribusiness (see below). As table 4.3 indicates, there are some extremely large holdings in the UK, and the average farm size is three times that within the EEC as a whole.

From this table, we can see that there are still a large number of farms below 300 acres, and that about half the cultivated acreage

Table 4.3   Land holdings in the UK, 1974

Acreage	Number of holdings	%	Acres	%
¼ to 299	189,000	91.6	13.8m	57.9
300 and above	17,700	8.5	9.9m	42.1

is worked by small farmers. However, this also means that there are some very large land holdings, and that nearly 10 million acres are farmed by only 17,700 farms/firms.

This leads us on to the second point, in so far as large holdings become attractive to investors, who would not be prepared to buy up small units, but who are keen to purchase large acreages as long-term financial speculations. In the UK, the growth of pension funds has meant that there is a constant source of investment capital for safe sectors: the networks of government support mean that agriculture is far less risky than, for example, industry of most types. As table 4.4 indicates, institutional holdings of land are now important – and they will also be owners who are happy to increase profitability by dealing with fellow corporations in the shape of agribusiness.

Table 4.4   Holdings of land in Great Britain

Body	Acreage
Local authorities	929,559
Nationalised industries	359,233
Crown	325,055
Conservation trusts	201,452
Universities	180,385
Financial institutions	170,000
Church	157,814
Government	121,663
(excl. MAFF	28,112
Forestry Commission	80,555

Both these trends impinge upon the third change, which is the changing nature of rural ED and land-use. Apart from the changing costs of transportation, a situation in which the farmer contracts with large firms for the whole of a crop, and then sees that firm arrive with harvesters and depart for the processing plant with the crop, is obviously very different from that discussed by von Thünen. This arrival of the market at the farm gates, plus the availability of chemical inputs, makes a nonsense of the notion of sharply differentiated land-use zones. The same is true for what has always been marginal land, for technological change is threatening to alter this too. In the past, sheep have normally been a major feature of upland farming, because they cannot be reared indoors under intensive conditions. However, the recent development of the so-called Cambridge sheep, which can be produced under battery conditions, promises to remove even this aspect of specialisation. Under such conditions, it is likely that even more upland will disappear beneath forest, whence it came.

4.5 Implications

All in all then, we can see that ED within the countryside is undergoing major transformations. The delicate balance that once existed between people and nature is being rapidly replaced by intensive agricultural-cum-industrial activity. Of course, farming was always conditioned by economic considerations, but as we have seen, these are now paramount for an increasing number of producers; as figure 4.4 implies, this also has major *social* implications for rural areas.

Key issues

ECONOMIC RENT The term economic rent relates to the advantages that one piece of land has in relation to another. In other words, land near to the market will produce a higher economic rent than land far away, because we do not have to take transport costs into account. Similarly, an increase in fertility would improve economic rent, although von Thünen did not include such variations. Note that economic rent will become difficult to determine very close to the urban market, as there urban land-uses will be in competition; (the same remarks apply to bid-rents on the rural fringe: there agricultural uses will compete with residential ones; see figure 3.1(c)).

INTEGRATION Integration can be thought of as a latter day development of the principle of agglomeration (see chapter 3). Spatial concentrations are now less important than integrations, whereby a corporation has control of its inputs and outputs. Sometimes a large firm will simply arrange numerous contracts with suppliers (this has always been a feature of the car industry) but a more sophisticated approach involves creating or buying up existing firms, in order to be able to control more and more aspects of the production process. One obvious advantage of such

"We've gone back to the Three-Field System—one belongs to an Arab, one to a Dutchman and one to a pension fund."

Figure 4.4   Changing values in the countryside (courtesy of Punch)

growth is that larger firms are less inclined to be affected by price changes than small ones: very large firms can dictate their own prices.

AGRICULTURAL SUPPORTS The relationship between supply and demand in the agricultural market-place is highly complex, due to the intervention of governments. In Britain, there has been a long history of subsidies for farmers, with grants being given to improve the quality of farm stock, or to bring land into cultivation. Governments gave these grants to farmers in order to improve domestic agriculture, and thus reduce the costs of importing food. Since our entry into the EEC, many of these supports have changed, because Europe as a whole *over*-produces some foodstuffs. In consequence, farmers will actually be paid *not* to produce some substances, and EEC surpluses are disposed of (to non-developed countries, or to Russia, for instance), rather than allowing prices to fall through overproduction.

5
The political context

5.1 The nature of political economy

In this volume we have tried to examine the ways in which the
process of economic development takes place in different contexts:
in regions, in cities, and in rural areas. Our argument has shown
clearly that many of the models that we as geographers use can
provide only partial information about ED. This is because they
focus upon individual decision makers, and tend to forget about
the wider world. This means that it is not always useful to focus
upon the decisions made by single firms or homeowners, without
also taking into account the society within which they function.
This means that land-use patterns can only be understood by also
evaluating the large number of social and political matters which
impinge upon behaviour: in short, we need to understand not
simply economic behaviour, but the *political-economy* of behaviour.
Within capitalist societies like our own, a political economy
approach reminds us to focus upon the housing market or the role
of pension funds. In different countries, different issues would be
of importance: thus in South Africa, for instance, the process of ED
in residential areas is shaped by ethnic issues as much as by other
considerations. A land-use model which did not recognise the
constraints of apartheid would consequently by valueless.

5.2 The ice cream salesperson problem

To illustrate this point, let us refer to another classic economic
model, that of Hotelling. It deals with a simple problem, namely
the location of firms along a strip of territory. It is usually called
the ice cream vendor model, in that it can be applied readily to ED
along a beach or similar area. This may seem a fairly simple problem, but it is more intricate than one might suppose. Under
conditions of free competition, the model predicts that two vendors
will stand back to back on the beach, as near as possible to the
middle point. Only in this way can they guarantee that the

competitor will not try to edge forward and increase his or her sales area.

Hotelling assumed that such organisation would be the logical outcome of free competition. But what about planning restriction? What about private beaches, owned by hotels? What about rationalisation, which means that there is only one firm still in business selling what now passes for ice 'cream'?

We might also ask; how much of this rational pattern of ED is governed by broader political considerations? We include a lengthy extract from sociologist and geographer Ray Pahl (1975, pp. 304–6), which reminds us that these wider contexts are always important.

Let us assume in all cases a warm sunny day, a sandy beach and people of all ages scattered fairly regularly along it. The problem is to provide them with ice cream under capitalist, socialist and Maoist principles. What distributive system would serve each power structure most appropriately and how would the spatial forms vary?

In the capitalist system the state has passed legislation preventing a monoploy. Thus two ice-cream-sellers are on the beach. There may have been more smaller operators offering ice cream of various sorts and qualities in the past. Over time, however, as a result of mergers, takeovers and bankruptcies only the two remain. Each is unwilling to allow the other to have access to any market in which the one might gain at the expense of the other. Hence, whilst it might be more convenient for the customer to have an ice-cream-seller closer than half a beach-length away, neither capitalist operator is prepared to move away from the centre point of the beach. To do so would risk losing more than half the market. The consequences of such an arrangement would probably be tacit price-fixing agreements. The state would tend to support the spatial pattern by directing the access road and by concentrating other beach facilities to the centre point. The effect of this would be to attract a higher concentration of population, especially those with young children, towards the centre of the beach. This, in turn, would encourage vendors of other commodities eagerly seeking the opportunities for making profits.

Under socialism such territorial injustice would not be countenanced. Given that no extra resources can be devoted to the distribution of ice cream in the early years, it nevertheless seems necessary to decentralise in order to improve the accessibility structure for those on the ends of the beach. The socialist planners conclude that each ice cream outlet should be two thirds of the way along the beach. In this way no one will be more than a third of a beach-length away from ice cream, as opposed to the possibility of half a beach-length under capitalism. In order to be sure that each ice cream seller has exactly the same quality of product, the state would probably employ a quality-checker to make sure that the fixed price-level guaranteed a standard quality. Since the wages of the ice cream sellers would not be related to the amount of ice cream sold there would be a danger that some sellers would prefer to go swimming than to stay in the stuffy ice cream dispensing hut. There might therefore be temptations to reduce stock or price in order to sell out more quickly and thus gain more leisure time. The fertile minds of the two vendors might devise more ingenious ways of working the system to their advantage by various forms of collusion. The state system of checking might have to be increased in the absence of genuine socialist consciousness amongst the state ice cream vendors. This might increase the cost of ice cream. In order to economise it might be necessary to have but one ice cream seller who would obviously move to the centre of the beach. The young people would say that the old territorial injustices of capitalism had reappeared.

Under Maoist Communism the whole notion of state-controlled ice cream manufacture and distribution is open to question. The people can make their own ice cream: let a hundred flavours freeze! By contriving ingenious methods of insulation with old newspapers, a simple mass-produced thermos container is devised and each family is able to have its own supply of ice cream on the beach. All take their turn at making ice cream – but some unhappy families with incompetent ice-cream-makers rarely taste anything resembling the commodity it is understood once existed under other political systems. Nevertheless, despite a wide variation in the quality of the homely ice cream, the people believe that there is no inequality of the *distribution* of ice cream and they are content with their system of territorial justice for a time. However, some of the younger people, who taste the various sorts of home-made ice cream as they make comradely contact with their fellows, begin to consider it unfair that some families should provide themselves with privileged taste-sensations. Clearly injustice does exist: some ice cream is better than others.

There is no alternative but to forbid the consumption of ice cream on the beach in the interests of egalitarian principles and for the good of all. Water quenches thirst better and is also better for health. Unfortunately, there is only one water tap on the beach and it is exactly in the middle. The people wisely decide to erect a public convenience close to the tap. Other facilities, such as a store for beach shades, are put at the central location.

In time, as the people become more prosperous they start to complain ... The young people want ice cream ... An old woman who remembers the recipe sets up a stall...

5.3 Economic development in different contexts

Let us now build upon Pahl's outlines with a brief examination of ED within different political economies; we take as our examples the very different cases of South Africa, the USSR and China.

(a) South Africa

It is now generally understood that South Africa occupies a unique position within the world economy. Although it is aggressively anti-communist, many other capitalist nations have relatively few formal links with its political, economic or sporting representatives. The reason for this is the country's expressed policy of *separate development*, or apartheid, as it is more usually termed. This does not simply mean that residential segregation within cities is based upon racial rather than economic grounds, or that the different races possess very different civil rights. It also effectively means that the whole process of ED within South Africa is now geared to the aims of separate racial development. This is outlined by David Smith (1978, p. 87):

> the policy of apartheid in South Africa involves the creation of race–space homogeneity. All land is allocated for the exclusive occupation of one of the officially recognised race groups – the Africans (Blacks or Bantu), Asians (mainly Indians), Coloureds and Whites. The national strategy is for the creation of 'Home-lands' or 'Bantustans' for the Africans, leaving the majority of the country (about 86% of the surface area) for the Whites. The Indian and Coloured people have no Homelands and are being 'encouraged' to concentrate in certain designated towns. Within the cities, each race has its own strictly segregated 'Group Areas'.
>
> The creation of this tidy racial geography necessitates the involuntary movement of large numbers of people. By the end of 1975 the Groups Areas Act had required the resettlement of 465,393 people (305,739 Coloureds, 153,756 Asians and 5898 Whites); the total number of Africans moved ... is not known precisely, but is generally estimated at well over one million.

In order to make these transfers effective, the South African government has developed in addition a policy of economic development, which is focused upon 20 growth centres: these are shown

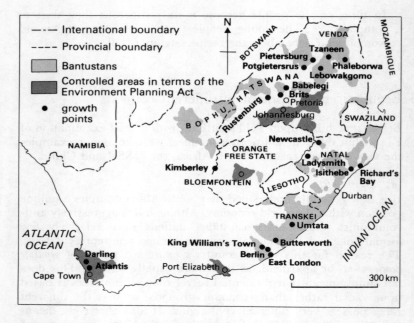

Figure 5.1   Growth points and controlled areas in terms of the Environment Planning Act, South Africa

in figure 5.1. Following the Environment Planning Acts in 1967, the state now possesses industrial legislation which is a grotesque parody of the measures traditionally employed in the UK (see again, for example, book 1). In South Africa, the development of industry is restricted, not by the size of the factory, but by the firm's racial composition: the Black–White ratio must not exceed 2:1. Conversely, in the Homelands, the incentives for firms to relocate revolve around the absence of legislation determining minimum wage levels, and poorer working conditions for the workers (which again reduce the costs of labour); these include fewer holidays, less sick leave and a longer working week. As one South African geographer observes, 'as long as the objective of stemming Black influx into the white areas remains the pivot of the whole programme for spatial industrial change, so long must Blacks suffer the continuing burdens of mounting unemployment, poverty-in-employment and miserable work environments under apartheid' (Rogerson, 1982, p. 63).

(b.)   USSR
If the policy of ED in South Africa is a mix of state control and capitalist development, the situation in the USSR is very

different. There state control is virtually complete, and the economic system is just one of the sectors over which this control is exercised. Although some writers have termed this 'state capitalism' (and as we have seen, the Soviet Union does undertake a great deal of trade with capitalist nations: along with South Africa, it is one of the largest producers of the world's gold, for instance), the economic system in the USSR is in reality very different from those that we have examined in the UK and USA. Effectively, all citizens work for the state (and are obliged to do so), are in receipt of state housing, and may be dispatched to different jobs and different regions if required. Equally, the state is not constrained to produce consumer goods, but can concentrate upon the production of heavy industrial products, engineering and agriculture.

The patterns of ED within the country as a whole, and within the different Republics that make up the USSR, is also centrally dictated. As one political geographer shows, quite specific – and often non-economic – criteria have been employed. Mellor writes of the pre-war period (1982, pp. 126–7):

> Marxist–Leninist doctrine stressing equalisation of regional development stimulated interest in the eastern regions, reflected in the *Ural–Kuzbass Kombinat*, the opening up of the Karaganda coalfield and the stategically motivated Komsomolsk steelworks in the Far East. Siberia was also secretively remote, appealing to strategic interests and to the planners' concept of a closed economy . . . The Second World War gave further impetus to the strategic shift of industry into the eastern regions as plants were hurriedly moved to escape the invading Germans . . . Few of the evacuated plants were to return to their old sites in European Russia, which were completely re-equipped.
>
> Under Stalin, little change was made to economic strategy in the post-war years and in a way rehabilitation of wartime damage called for the same approach as after the civil war, with emphasis upon heavy capital goods for reconstruction . . . After Stalin's death in 1953 there was a slow change, and . . . the Soviet authorities became less obsessed with concern for a closed and self-sufficient economy . . . At the same time there has been increasing discussion of the best ways of organising the economy, with ideas swinging between decentralisation (under Krushchev) to a return to a more centralised form (under Brezhnev), though neither seems to have reached the desired goal.

In short, Soviet ED policy has been a struggle between ideological pressures and stategic needs on the one hand, and the problems of opening up the hostile regions to the East. Marxist–Leninist doctrine states that communist ideology should be spread vigorously and that resources, both physical and human, should also be fully developed (the concepts of agricultural margins would not be recognised in such situations for example: see chapter 4). For this reason, planned developments such as the Ural–Kuzbass iron and steel complex emerged, in which the problems of production spread over several hundred kilometres were simply ignored. Similarly, the strategic weakness of the western frontiers, which were overrun in 1917 and 1941, has encouraged ED in the east, despite the poorly developed infrastructures there, the transportation problems, the shortages of skilled labour and the harsh physical environment. In short, state capitalism can emphasise the spatial aspects of ED at the expense of profit.

(c) People's Republic of China

The contrast between the USSR and the capitalist nations is thus extreme. A further interesting footnote can be added if we also examine ED in mainland China. This experienced a revolution in 1949, and began to develop a highly centralised state socialist economy along Soviet lines. Five-year plans were produced and 694 major factories throughout the country were planned. In 1958, however, Mao proposed the 'Great Leap Forward', which was essentially an expression of communist belief. Instead of highly centralised production, the focus was instead to rest upon the smallest units of Chinese life, the communes. These were to become responsible for their own industrial production wherever possible, and farmers were encouraged to leave the fields and begin smelting and welding. One of Mao's basic beliefs, in the importance of individual struggle, was put into practice.

This bold experiment in redefining the basics of ED were shattered by various natural calamities and the withdrawal of Soviet aid in 1960. Since that time, the move towards central control has been reasserted, despite the further struggles that took place during the Cultural Revolution in 1966–69. Once more, we see the contradictions that can emerge between political philosophies, which may dictate a certain pattern or organisation, such as decentralisation, and the harsh economic realities which dictate specialisation and concentration of production.

5.4 Conclusions

In this chapter, we have tried to round off our discussion of ED with several examples that underline a basic fact: namely that although economic activity operates within certain basic rules and frameworks, these are always open to manipulation by society and the state. In some countries, the aims are clear: a particular political ideology dictates the way in which development is permitted to take place. In others, the intentions are less obvious. As a final question, we ask: what are the political and social intentions operating within Britain, and how have they shaped the patterns of ED as a result?

Photographic section

1 Mills at Saltaire, Bingley, Yorkshire

The emergence of industrial capitalism in the early nineteenth century produced entirely new developments on the economic landscape. Factories were initially free-standing, dependent upon raw materials or power sources rather than urban labour forces, as happened later. Titus Salt's mill complex in West Yorkshire was such a development, utilising local fibres and canal transportation. Salt also built model homes for his workers, and founded thereby a new settlement, Saltaire. His philanthropy did not extend, however, to the provision of any public houses in the new community.

2 Mitchell's Plain, a new town in South Africa

The path of economic development has been very different in different countries, despite Rostow's predictions. Political influences are powerful, as in South Africa for example. There, the principles of *separate development* – apartheid, as it is called in Afrikaans – dictate the duplication of black and white economic and social structures. Mitchell's Plain is a New Town out on False Bay to the southeast of Cape Town, catering solely for Cape Coloureds. By 1984, the population will be 250,000, many attracted by advertising slogans such as 'Where your children grow up determines their future'. Housing is expensive, however, and the remoteness of the town (27 kilometres from Cape Town) limits employment opportunities.

3 The bakery in the Findus plant at Longbenton, Tyne and Wear

Branch plants in peripheral regions may bring new jobs, but these are usually few in number and low in skills. This Findus development, discussed in the text, was intended to produce pizzas, although local political leaders are now concerned that the company will close down other plants, in neighbouring regions with a history of union activity, and relocate the production lines in Longbenton.

4 Britannic House, British Petroleum's head office in London

Multinational corporations now wield enormous power, both at home and abroad. Each day they make decisions involving billions of pounds or dollars and affecting millions of people. They are major employers, and their decisions to locate in one country or another, or even one city as opposed to another, can have major implications for patterns of national and/or regional economic development. It is not surprising that, despite high land costs, London still boasts a major concentration of prestigious headquarters for companies with multinational functions, like this block belonging to British Petroleum. Many commentators argue that until such companies are prepared to relocate to Newcastle or Liverpool, attempts to boost regional economies are doomed to failure.

5 The Trans Alaska oil pipeline, in which BP has an interest, at Squirrel Creek

As noted in caption 4, multinationals frequently spread their operations across dozens of countries. In this way, they can exploit cheap labour resources, tax incentives and local markets, whilst at the same time minimising the risk of warfare or coup d'état by spreading it across many undertakings. Nor should it be forgotten that these firms are truly international. Their activities are not constrained by political boundaries, and only Albania has truly resisted their incursions. A pipeline like this one has recently been completed between the Soviet Union and Western Europe and is just one manisfestation of the 'Vodka-Cola trade', in which firms like BP are involved.

6 Greeley, Colorado, an example of 'agribusiness'

Although this photograph may appear more typical of a steel mill or a car plant, it is in reality the heart of a cattle ranch at Greeley, some 70 miles from Denver, Colorado. The operator is using remote control to fill a truck with feed, and she will then dispatch it to the proper pen. Note the ways in which agribusiness has changed the whole social organisation of farming. It has employed women in responsible tasks, and connected the rhythms of agriculture to those of the stock market rather than the seasons. It is astonishing to realise that there are now fewer farms in the USA than there were in 1870, before the westward expansion really got under way, and that these new, large holdings are in fact sophisticated businesses: a recent report discusses a 3,500 acre farm where one man manages a turnover of $3.5 million each year, and is responsible for $500,000 of machinery – much of it of the sort seen here.

Photograph 1   Mills at Saltaire, Bingley, Yorkshire

Photograph 2   Mitchell's Plain, a new town in South Africa

hotograph 3   The bakery in the Findus plant at Longbenton, Tyne and Wear

Photograph 4   Britannic House, British Petroleum's head office in London

Photograph 5 The Trans Alaska oil pipeline, in which BP has an interest, at Squirrel Creek

Photograph 6   Greeley, Colorado, an example of 'agribusiness'

References

Abler, R., Adams, J. and Gould, P. (1971), *Spatial Organisation*, Prentice Hall, Englewood Cliffs.

Dicken, P. and Lloyd, P. (1981), *Modern Western Society*, Harper and Row, London.

Geofile (1982), *The 31 least developed countries*, Elizabeth Wearer Ltd.

Haas, E., Kates, R. and Bowden, M (1977). *Reconstruction following disaster*, MIT Press, Cambridge Massachusetts.

Keeble, D. (1976), *Industrial location and planning in the UK*, Methuen, London.

Keeble, D. (1981), 'Deindustrialisation means unemployment', *Geographical Magazine*, **53** (7), 458–464.

Kidron, M. and Segal, M. (1981), *State of the World Atlas*, Pluto Press, London.

Lee, R. (1976), 'Integrations, spatial structure and the capitalist mode of production in the EEC', in Lee, R. and Ogden, P. E. (eds) *Economy and Society in the EEC*, Saxon House, Farnborough.

Lloyd, P. and Reeve, D. E. (1982), 'N.W. England 1971–77: a study in industrial decline and economic restructuring', *Regional Studies*, **16**(5).

Mellor, R. E. H. (1982), *The Soviet Union and its geographical problems*, Macmillan, London.

Newby, H. (1979), *Green and pleasant land?*, Penguin, Harmondsworth.

Newby, H. and Utting, P. (1982), 'Agribusiness in the UK: social and political implications', unpublished ms, Department of Sociology, University of Essex.

Pahl, R. E. (1975), *Whose City?*, Penguin, Harmondsworth.

Peet, R. (1969), 'The spatial expansion of commercial agriculture in the nineteenth century', *Economic Geography*, **45**, 283–301.

Robson, B. (1982), 'The Bodley barricade', Chapter 3 in Cox, K. and Johnston, R. J. (eds), *Conflict, Politics and the Urban Scene*, Longman, Harlow.

Rogerson, C. M. (1982), 'Apartheid, decentralisation and spatial industrial change', in Smith, D. M. (ed), *Living under Apartheid*, Allen & Unwin, London, 47–63.

Rostow, W. W. (1960), *The stages of economic growth*, Cambridge University Press.

Smith, D. M. (1978), 'Involuntary population movement in South Africa', *Area*, **10**(2), 87–89.

Weber, A. (1909), *Uber den Standorten der Industrien*, trans. as 'Alfred Weber's theory of the location of industries', by Friedrich, C. J. (1929), University of Chicago Press.